Prayers for Life

RENA BOSTON

For licensing/copyright information, for additional copies, or for
use in specialized settings, contact:

Just Writers Publishing Company
"Where Fingers Write From The Heart"
Round Lake, Illinois 60073
(847) 494-8420 (telephone)
www.justwriters.com
renaboston@comcast.net
justwriters@comcast.net

Pray

Pray

Pray

This special dedication is given to JANET LAKE, my sister and friend. It is in recognition of her dedication and perseverance in promoting the *Jehovah, It's All About YOU* book and compact disc. For this reason, it is only appropriate that I especially dedicate this *Prayers for Life* book to her.

Thank you, Janet, with all my love!
~Rena

ACKNOWLEDGMENTS

In Memory of
Arthur and Virginia Boston Sr.

Special Thanks
Bishop Michael Cole
Dr. Carlis L. Moody Sr.
Mrs. Mary A. Moody
Dr. Randolph W. Moore
Elder Edward Jackson
Lisa Laudé-Raymond
Inez Jones
Delois Robinson
Mary Howard
Cassandra Mitchell
Julianna Taylor
Alleen Miller

To all who encouraged me, I love you very much.

Foreword

AS A PASTOR, I have come to realize the development time of God's "calling" is divinely specific. To properly discern the season that we are in, one has to be strongly connected in prayer. In my many years of traveling the Mission Fields of the Nations, it has brought me to a clear and decisive truth, "Prayer is Powerful." I recall the times when my mind just didn't "get" what I needed to do, but when I tapped into the intercessory reserves of God, I found myself soaring and rendezvousing with the destiny God had created and prepared for me. I'm not saying that it was as easy as a piece of cake, but I am saying that life's tests and challenges presented on the Mission Fields were worth the personal and spiritual growth I gained along the journey. Through prayer, this type of power continues until today.

I congratulate Rena because she has certainly captured the true and timeless essence of the Glory of God experienced within the realm of the Holy Spirit as pertaining to this life and our experience of Divine Prayer. With this being said, we can truly confess that in the presence of the Lord is Divine Refuge. I know you will be blessed and challenged into a deeper relationship as you encounter these proven foundational depths of prayer.

Bishop Michael R. Cole,
Prelate North Dakota Jurisdiction,
Church of God in Christ

Especially for You:

_____

_____

_____

_____

_____

_____

2 Chronicles 7:14
If my people, which are called by my name, shall humble themselves, and pray, and seek my face, and turn from their wicked ways; then will I hear from heaven, and will forgive their sin, and will heal their land.

Matthew 18:18
Verily I say unto you, Whatsoever ye shall bind on earth shall be bound in heaven: and whatsoever ye shall loose on earth shall be loosed in heaven.

Mark 11:24
Therefore I say unto you, What things soever ye desire, when ye pray, believe that ye receive them, and ye shall have them.

Introduction

THIS *PRAYERS FOR LIFE* BOOK is written to promote prayer in our daily lives. Some people find it difficult to pray. Others say they don't know how to pray. Then, there are those, who desire their prayers to be elevated to a higher level.

This book promises to meet the specific need of each group. The only thing required is, to open your mouth and read/pray the prayer. Have a conversation with God. He will speak, and you can respond. You can speak, and he will respond. Rest your head upon his shoulder and discover: Prayer relaxes you!

The prayers contained in this book are fully scripted Bible-based, faith-filled prayers. However, they can be used as templates, as your faith moves you further into your prayer. God's Word encourages us to always pray, so we won't faint. Prayer is to our spirit, what breath is to the body; LIFE!

You are encouraged to pray these prayers until they become a part of you. They will help you live victoriously, if you engage them before you panic, doubt, or become fearful. Prayer changes people, things, and situations.

As you pray these prayers, I challenge you, to add your own heart and spirit, to them. They are LIFE, to those who pray them.

The Altar of Sacrifice

HISTORICALLY, SACRIFICES OFFERED TO GOD WERE ANIMALS that were pure, and without blemish. These sacrifices were used to reverence God, and get his attention/forgiveness. Prayer has replaced the need for animal sacrifices. We, our bodies, are the living sacrifice, which God accepts.

As we lay our hearts before God, on the Altar of Prayer, he grants us access into his presence. And when we pray according to his will, we can be confident that he hears us, and will answer us. He has promised that, before we call, he will answer and say, 'Here I Am'. Therefore, let us come boldly and regularly, to the Throne of God in prayer. When we come, we will receive his mercy and grace, which will help us, in our daily lives.

There is nothing mystical about prayer. Prayer is talking to God. While talking to him, we are also talking about him, about his promises, about others, and about ourselves. Try it! Just pray!

For example, let's talk to him, about him: "O Lord God, there is no God like you, in heaven or in the earth. You keep your promises to us. You show mercy to your servants. You uphold those, who walk before you with their whole heart. We bless you, Lord God Almighty. You have fulfilled that, which you have promised. You are a great God. You are sovereign. You cannot be contained. You are everywhere, at the same time. Let the truth of your Word be verified. Confirm your Word with miracles, signs, and wonders, in our lives."

We continue with our prayers of thanksgiving and praise, as we talk to him about others, and ourselves. All we have to do is, open our mouth and start talking. When we do that, we are laying our hearts, on The Altar of Sacrifice.

This book and the associated compact disc, contain prayers for almost any situation in life. Pray the prayers yourself, or listen to them being prayed. Use them to start, improve, or enhance your prayer life.

There is no need more critical today, than the need to know how to pray God's Word back to him. God will help us, as we yield ourselves to him.

Every intercessor should own a copy of this book!

Our Father

Our Father which art in heaven, hallowed be thy name. Thy kingdom come, thy will be done in earth, as it is in heaven. Give us this day our daily bread. And forgive us our debts, as we forgive our debtors. And lead us not into temptation, but deliver us from evil: For thine is the kingdom, and the power, and the glory, forever. Amen. (Matthew 6:9-13)

Father, in the name of Jesus, help us to become more intimately acquainted with you. You are:

OUR FATHER,
You are the Creator of all things. You are our Master and our Maker. You are the Ruler of our souls. You are our Father. Through the shed Blood of Jesus, we call you Father, Abba, Daddy. And as our Father, we can come to you, any time, day or night; and your ears are open to our cry.

WHICH ART IN HEAVEN,
Heaven is your throne, and the earth is your footstool. Heaven is your prepared place, for your prepared people. We rejoice knowing, that we will spend eternity with you. Our hearts and eyes are fixed on heaven, our eternal dwelling place.

HALLOWED BE THY NAME.
You are holy. We worship you in your holiness. We bow our hearts to you. Everything we need is in you. In you, all fullness dwell. Your name is holy. We reverence your name. Your names contain all that you are, and all that we need. You are:

Jehovah-Elohim	"The Eternal Creator"
Jehovah-Shammah	"The Lord Is Present"
Jehovah-Jireh	"The Lord Will Provide"
Adonai-Jehovah	"The Lord Our Sovereign"
Jehovah-Shalom	"The Lord Our Peace"
Jehovah-Nissi	"The Lord Our Banner"

Jehovah-Tsidkeenu	"The Lord Our Righteousness"
Jehovah-Saboath	"The Lord Of Hosts"
Jehovah-Eloheka	"The Lord Thy God"
Jehovah-Rohi	"The Lord My Shepherd"
Jehovah-Ropheka	"The Lord Our Healer"
Jehovah-Hoseenu	"The Lord Our Maker"
Jehovah-Elohay	"The Lord My God"
Jehovah-Elyon	"The Lord Most High"
Jehovah-Eloheenu	"The Lord Our God"
Jehovah-Mekaddishkem	"The Lord Our Sanctifier"

Our all-sufficiency is in your name.

THY KINGDOM COME,
Holy Spirit, take residence within us, that we may glorify God in our spirits, and in our bodies. We declare that God is the only, true and living God. He is Lord and King of our lives. Our God reigns. Let your manifested power be seen in the earth, through your people. Let your kingdom come in us.

THY WILL BE DONE IN EARTH, AS IT IS IN HEAVEN.
Let the people praise thee, O God, let the people praise thee. Let the earth be filled with your glory, even as heaven is filled. We decree and declare that every knee shall bow, and every tongue shall confess, that Jesus Christ is Lord, to the glory of God the Father. Let thy will be done in the earth, O God; let thy will be done. Let all who walk contrary to your will, come to an understanding of you. Illuminate the hearts and minds of your people everywhere; every tribe and every nation.

Let the fullness of your will be manifested in the earth. Draw sinners to repentance. Cause those who have not heard your Word, to hear, receive and obey. Bless your children to triumph in the earth.

GIVE US THIS DAY OUR DAILY BREAD.
Father, you know what we have need of, even before we ask. But you told us to

ask, and it shall be given; seek, and we shall find; knock, and it shall be opened unto us. You promised to supply all of our needs, according to your riches in glory. We thank you for blessing and sustaining us. We have no lack in you. We have all sufficiency, in all things.

AND FORGIVE US OUR DEBTS, AS WE FORGIVE OUR DEBTORS.
Father, let your love rule in our hearts. Your love will enable us to forgive, when others ask to be forgiven, and when they refuse to ask for forgiveness. Let your spirit sit on the throne of our hearts, directing us to always do that, which is good and right. Forgive us of all our trespasses, we pray.

AND LEAD US NOT INTO TEMPTATION, BUT DELIVER US FROM EVIL:
Father, we thank you for your provisions and your protection. You have blessed us and made us a blessing. Thank you that our life is not a stumbling block to onlookers.

FOR THINE IS THE KINGDOM, AND THE POWER, AND THE GLORY, FOR EVER.
Thine, O Lord is the greatness, and the power, and the glory, and the victory, and the majesty; for all that is in the heaven and in the earth is thine. Thine is the kingdom, O Lord, and thou art exalted as head above all.

AMEN.
It is so! Let it be so! So be it!

Table of Contents

Entrance

It is important that we pray regularly. This book is designed to encourage and motivate daily prayer. Although we tried, but *words* can never really contain the personification of Jesus in his fullness. He is so vast! Nevertheless, a thorough research of the names given to Jesus was conducted to provide a glimpse of who he is. Several sources were used; however, the names included are names confirmed by the Word of God. Be blessed, as you bless the Name of Jesus.

Jesus' Name 1

FATHER, we come before your throne, in the wonderful name of Jesus. Let the earth be silent, and stand still in awe of him. His name is great, and greatly to be praised.

JESUS:
The Holy One
The Only Begotten Son of God
The Elect of God
The Just One

JESUS:
The Lord of Glory
The Lord our Righteousness
The Lord of Hosts
The Lord of Heaven and Earth

JESUS:
The Judge of all the Earth
The Lion of the Tribe of Judah
The Author and Finisher of our Faith
The King of kings

JESUS!

Father, you are our God, the Almighty! You open your hand and satisfy every living thing. You are true and faithful. You fulfill your promises to your people. You watch over your Word to perform it. You hasten your Word, and cause it to produce fruit in our lives. In Jesus' name we thank you. Amen!

Jesus' Name II

FATHER, we come to you in the powerful name of Jesus. At his name, Satan trembles and demons flee. There is power in the name of Jesus.

JESUS:
The Lord of lords
The Savior of the world
Our Advocate with the Father
The Bridegroom

JESUS:
The Friend that sticks closer than any brother
The Way, the Truth and the Life
The Light of the world
The Bread of Life

JESUS:
The Living Water
The Door
The Lamb of God
Emmanuel, God with us

JESUS!

Father, you are the God of Abraham, Isaac, and Jacob. And you are our God, our Lord, and Savior! You redeemed our life from destruction. You have done for us that which no man could do. We are the work of your hands and we glorify your name. Amen.

Jesus' Name III

FATHER, in the mighty name of Jesus, we come before your throne. There is supernatural power in the name of Jesus. We worship and honor the miracle working power contained in His name, Jesus, the Son of God.

JESUS:
Our Master
Our Redeemer
The True Vine
A Sure Foundation

JESUS:
The Rock of Ages
Our Messiah
Our Deliverer
The Prince of Peace

JESUS:
The Rose of Sharon
The Bright and Morning Star
The Alpha and the Omega
The Beginning and the Ending
The First and the Last

JESUS:
He who was, is, and is to come
The Lilly of the Valley
The Resurrection and the Life
The Stone that the builders rejected
The Chief Corner Stone

JESUS!

Father, we bless the name of our Lord and Savior; the name which is above every name, the name that the righteous run into and are safe, the name that gives rest to the weary soul, and strength to those who have no strength. The name of Jesus!

Jesus, you are our hiding place. You are with us in the fire. You are with us in the valley of the shadow of death. And, you are with us on the mountaintop. Jesus, you are our solid foundation, and we thank you. It is in your name, we pray. Amen!

The Living Word 1

FATHER, I am blessed, because:

- I walk in your favor,
- I declare your judgments, and,
- I delight in your statutes.

I am blessed, because:

- I am covered by you,
- I rejoice in your way, and,
- I meditate on your goodness.

I am blessed!

I am chosen because I seek you with my whole heart.
I am free because I take heed to your Word.
All of my ways are directed to keep your statutes.
I arise early to seek your face to keep me from stumbling.
I keep my feet from evil so I can live a quiet and peaceable life.
I keep my eyes holy, as I behold your wondrous works, in all the earth.
I turn my heart and my eyes away from vanity.
I diligently pursue you, because I long for your presence.
Father, thank you for your sustaining Word!
All these confessions, I make, in the name of Jesus Christ of Nazareth. Amen.

The Living Word II

FATHER, I love your Word.

Your Word is true from the beginning to the end.
The entrance of your Word gives light.
Your Word is pure, and it cleanses my heart.
Your Word is sweeter than honey to my mouth.
Your Word is hidden in my heart, that I might not sin against you.
Your Word is the meditation of my heart, day and night.
Your Word has made me wiser than mine enemies.
Your Word has increased my understanding of life.
Your Word is a lamp unto my feet, and a light unto my path.
Your Word examines and judges me.
Every one of your righteous judgments endures forever.
I have not departed from your judgments, for you have taught me what is good
and what is right.
Your testimonies are the rejoicing of my heart.

Father, I thank you that your Word has kept me. Your Word has maintained my life. You protect me, and guard everything concerning me. It is in Jesus' name, I make these confessions according to your Word. Amen!

The Living Word III

FATHER, in the name of Jesus, I ask you to order my footsteps in your Word, so iniquity won't have any dominion over me.

According to your loving-kindness, let your Word forever be alive within me. Let my heart stand in awe of your Word.

I rejoice at thy Word, as one that finds great spoil.

Let the words of my mouth, and the meditation of my heart, be acceptable in your sight. Because your righteousness is an everlasting righteousness, and your law is Truth.

I decree and declare: "Great peace have they which love your law: and nothing shall offend them." Father, you are my hiding place and my shield of protection.

My hope is in your Word. Uphold me according to your Word that I may live and not be ashamed of my hope. Hold me up and I shall be safe.

Deal with me according to your mercy, and teach me your statutes.

Let your face shine upon me that I might walk in your light.

I will praise you with an upright heart. Several times a day I will praise you, because of your righteous judgments.

Father, I decree and declare, these truths are being manifested in my life every day. In Jesus' name, amen!

Speak It

FATHER, in the name of Jesus, I thank you for opening doors which were closed to me. Thank you for closing doors that were no longer benefitting me. Thank you for directing my footsteps, and giving me the wisdom to move forward.

I call forth those things you have preserved for me. I call them forth in their fullness. They are manifested this day in my life.

I walk into my wealthy place, and I dwell there continually.

I walk upon my high places. I take back every thing the devil has stolen from me. I speak resurrected life to the things he killed in my life. Everything the enemy destroyed in my life is rebuilt, by the Spirit of God.

I decree and declare that my ministry is led by the Spirit of God.

I decree and declare my emotional and physical health are in their fullness.

My home and my marriage are operating in the peace of God.

My decisions are righteous and full of wisdom.

I decree and declare, my parents, grandparents, and siblings are living in their fullness. My children and grandchildren are obeying the Word of God in its fullness. My friends and other relationships are chosen by God, and our hearts are in unity.

I decree and declare, my finances are blessed and in their fullness. All of my mortgages and debts are paid-in-full or supernaturally canceled. My businesses and jobs are in their fullness.

In the name of Jesus Christ, my Lord and Savior, I cancel every plot, plan, scheme and strategy that the enemy has devised against me. I decree and declare, "No weapon formed against me will prosper."

I speak life into every dead situation. I speak the resurrection power of God into every life situation that I might face.

I am blessed and highly favored. Thank you Father for "Your Favor." Thank you for being the center of my life. In Jesus' name I pray. Amen, it is so!

The Heart

A good man out of the good treasure of the heart brings forth good things, and an evil man out of the evil treasure of the heart brings forth evil things. Blessed are the pure in heart for they shall see God.

Love 1

FATHER, in the name of Jesus, we thank you, that the 'Fruit of the Spirit' abides within us. We walk in the spirit of love, joy, peace, longsuffering, gentleness, goodness, faith, meekness, and temperance. We rest in your love. You so loved us that you gave your only son to die on the cross for our sins. We thank you for your abounding love.

Even as you loved us, help us to love one another. Cause us to realize, the more we genuinely love one another, the more your glory will be revealed.

You said, "For I know the thoughts that I think toward you. Thoughts of peace, and not of evil, to give you an expected end." There is so much you desire to do for us, if we would only fortify ourselves in love. Don't let us lose our focus. Enlighten our hearts to know that it is for our good, to walk in love. Love is what will help us reach our expected end. Purge our hearts and make us acceptable for your use. We decree and declare, we have departed from evil and we now pursue love.

Father, as you are, so are we in this world. You are love; and we decree and declare, we are vessels of your love in the earth. We are epistles seen and read of men. Let the life we live, speak love. Don't let our life darken the words on the pages of your Holy Bible. Don't let us become a stumbling block.

We decree and declare, our children's love for you will grow as they grow. They will not turn their hearts away from you. They will meditate on your Word day and night.

We decree and declare, Satan is defeated in the lives of our children, our grandchildren, and our generations to come.

Father, thank you, that your love has lifted us up. When nothing else could help, your love came. We will show you our gratitude by walking in love.

Because we know when we walk in love, the wicked one cannot touch us. In Jesus' name, amen.

Love II

FATHER, your Word says, "Though I speak with the tongues of men and of angels, and have not charity, I am become as sounding brass, or a tinkling cymbal. And though I have the gift of prophecy, and understand all mysteries, and all knowledge; and though I have all faith so that I could remove mountains, and have not charity, I am nothing. And though I bestow all my goods to feed the poor, and though I give my body to be burned, and have not charity, it profits me nothing."

Father, in the name of Jesus, teach us to honor you, by loving one another. Don't let us deceive ourselves in thinking that our good deeds, and our sacrifices, can replace your commandment to love.

You said, "When we operate in your love, we are patient and kind. And we will endure the just and unjust sufferings, which are placed upon us." You said, "We will neither envy others nor think more highly of ourselves, than we ought to."

We yield our hearts to you. Because when we allow your love to control us, we will walk and abide in love. We will carry ourselves in a manner, which will glorify you. We will not get upset and angry, easily.

Father, our hearts will rejoice in truth, we will think on things, which are true, honest, just, pure, lovely, and of a good report.

We resist the temptation, to play childish games. Our growth will not be stunt. We will grow up spiritually and naturally. We put aside childish ways, which hinder our development in love.

We thank you, that within our hearts abide faith, hope, and love; and we will allow love to have its perfect work in us. In Jesus' name, we pray. Amen!

Forgiveness 1

FATHER, in the name of Jesus, hear the prayer we pray before you this day. You said, "If my people, which are called by my name, shall humble themselves, and pray, and seek my face, and turn from their wicked ways; then will I hear from heaven, and will forgive their sin, and will heal their land."

Father, we stand before you totally transparent. You told us to come and bring the conditions of our hearts to you. Here we are before your throne, seeking help. You promised that your arms were outstretched to us, and your ears were open to our cry.

We come knowing, you already know:

when we were wronged,
when someone sinned against us, and,
when we were violated.

You already know we were lied on, and people hated us without a reason.

You also know we were falsely accused, and close friends turned against us.

And Father, we come knowing you see our challenges and our resentment, but most of all O God, you see the time which has been wasted, because we would not forgive. Open our eyes that we might see. Your spirit cannot dwell where there is unforgiveness.

We surrender the condition of our hearts to you. Regulate our hearts by your spirit. We need you. You are our life, and we can do nothing without you.

Forgive us of our transgressions, our sins, iniquities, and our secret faults. In Jesus' name we pray, amen.

Forgiveness II

FATHER, your Word says, "The heart is deceitful above all things, and desperately wicked: who can know it?" You alone know the heart of every living creature. Search us, and whatever is not pleasing, wash and cleanse us through your Word. Massage our hearts and enable us to forgive.

Cause us to know that our wounds won't heal, if we hold on to painful memories. Wash us through your Word, so we can be healed.

Lord Jesus, teach us to release the pain to you.
Teach us to cast all of our cares upon you.

We give you our broken hearts.
Erase the pain and restore wholeness to us.

We give you the walls that we have built up.
Help us tear them down, and remove them, so we can forgive.

With your help, we will not give power and strength to unforgiveness.
We will not cause our destiny to be delayed or destroyed.

We routinely pray, "Forgive us our trespasses; as we forgive those who trespass against us!" We want your forgiveness; therefore, we must forgive. We must obey your Word. You have called us to forgive; to turn the other cheek, and if necessary, to give our coat. Help us Lord, to forgive. In Jesus' name we pray, amen.

Forgiveness III

FATHER, we come into your presence thanking you for grace and mercy. It is because of your grace and mercy that we are not consumed.

Forgive us for our trespasses against our neighbors.
Forgive us for not loving our enemies.
Forgive us for not doing unto others, as we would have them do unto us.
Forgive us, of our sins toward you.

You promised, if we turn to you, pray and confess our sins, you would hear, forgive, and cleanse us.

Father, we come to you, the only way we know how. Receive us, and judge us according to your loving-kindness. Give to each of us according to our ways, because you know our hearts.

We decree and declare, we won't fret because of evildoers.
We decree and declare, vengeance belongs to you and you will repay.
We decree and declare, we will keep ourselves free from the bondage of unforgiveness.
We decree and declare we choose to forgive.
We rejoice, because we have the power to forgive.

Thank you for our freedom in you. You have broken the chains of bondage and loosed the shackles of unforgiveness. With a clean conscience, we now make a decision to forgive, in Jesus' name, amen.

Forgiveness IV

FATHER, in the name of Jesus, be glorified in every area of our lives. Everywhere we go let your presence be with us. Make us sensitive to the voice of the Holy Spirit.

We acknowledge that you are God! There is no God like you in heaven above, or on the earth beneath. Thank you for the mercy you have extended to those who walk upright before you.

You have seated us in heavenly places in Christ Jesus. You have raised us up, high above our circumstances. We tread upon the head of the enemy. He is under our feet.

We decree and declare we are victorious. We will run and not get weary. We will go where you send us.

We forgive everyone who has hurt or harmed us in any way. We release everyone who has wronged us. We forgive and release ourselves, of all involvement in hurting or harming anyone.

Father, take all of us; not just a part, take all of our heart. Give us a fresh heart-to-heart encounter with you. We commit ourselves wholly to you. Teach us the good way wherein we should walk. Send the latter rain upon the land where your people dwell. Give us light in darkness.

If famine, destruction, or sickness comes, or if the enemy attacks and steals our goods, when we call upon your name, we know you will answer us, by your grace.

Father, we thank you for rest. You have given your people rest. We thank you, that your promises to us have not failed.

As you were with our forefathers, you have been with us. We will stand still and see your salvation. In stillness, let your mercy and grace rest upon us. In Jesus' name we pray, amen.

Peace 1

FATHER, in the name of Jesus, we decree and declare, we have the peace of God.

In the world, there are times of peace and times of war, but in you there is peace continually. We abide in peace, because you are our peace giver.

Your Word declares, "For unto us a child is born, unto us a son is given: and the government shall be upon his shoulder: and his name shall be called Wonderful, Counselor, the Mighty God, the Everlasting Father, and the Prince of Peace."

You are the Prince of Peace.
You are the head of the church. You are our Father.

You give light to those who sit in darkness. You lift up those who abide in the shadow of death. You guide our feet, and direct us into the pathway of peace.

Jesus, you said, "Peace I leave with you, my peace I give unto you: not as the world giveth, give I unto you. Let not your heart be troubled, neither let it be afraid."

Father, we thank you that worry and fear were abolished by your peace.

We release divine peace into our lives. We choose to abide in you, and let your Word abide in us. In this world we will have tribulation, but we will be of good cheer; because you have overcome the world. We thank you, that the victory you won, you gave it to us.

We will not fear! We decree and declare, though a host shall encamp against us, our hearts shall not fear. And if wars rise up against us, we are confident that we will win, because the Prince of Peace is on our SIDE. In Jesus' name we pray, amen.

Peace II

FATHER, thank you for giving us access to your throne. We come to give you thanks and to worship your name. We come because you are our life. Our peace is in you. We love and appreciate you.

We thank you, for lifting up your countenance upon us. We thank you, for giving us peace and truth in our innermost part. Our hearts have been renewed, through faith in your Word. Thank you for delivering our souls in peace, from the battles that were against us. We dwell in peace with those who hate us, and those who have wronged us. O God, when we do it your way, we lie down in peace and we sleep, because you make us to dwell, in safety.

Father, let your peace, which passes all understanding, keep our hearts and minds through Christ Jesus. We thank you for your abundant peace.

You said, "When a man's ways please you, you would make even his enemies to be at peace with him." We surrender our ways to you. We receive your divine peace.

Let us dwell continually in your perfect peace, as we trust you. Our hope is in you. You are the Prince of Peace.

You have ordained peace for us. You promised great peace to those who love your law, and nothing shall offend them. We decree and declare our children love your law. They are taught of the LORD, and great is their peace.

We thank you, because of Calvary we can go forth with joy, and walk in peace. We surrender our hearts to you. Let your peace rule in our hearts now and forevermore; in the name of Jesus we pray, amen.

Peace III

FATHER, in the name of Jesus, we thank you for peace. We thank you that the one who spoke to the wind and the waves, and said, "Peace be still" is on our side.

Our souls are not troubled, because our hope is in you! You shall fight for us, and we shall hold our peace.

The wicked walk in the imagination of their own heart, they are right in their own eyes, and they regard not the eyes of our God; who shall judge every man according to his doings.

But O God, when the wicked say, "Peace and Safety", then shall sudden destruction come upon them and they shall not escape.

Father, don't let us be deceived, or deceive ourselves, saying, "Peace, Peace", when there is no real peace, except in you.

Your Word declares, "The kingdom of God is not meat and drink; but righteousness, peace, and joy in the Holy Ghost." Thank you for the indwelling of the Holy Spirit, who leads, guides, and directs us.

Let every day we live be so precious, that we work to keep the unity of the Spirit, in the bond of peace.

You are not an author of confusion, but of peace.

Our feet carry the good news, the Gospel of peace.

We go in peace to the places you send us.

Our mouths bring forth good tidings, as we publish the peace of your salvation.

As we spread the good news of the Gospel, let hope generate in the hearts of those in despair, and let peace rest upon them.

You said, "Blessed are the peacemakers: for they shall be called the children of God." We decree that glory, honor, and peace, shall follow those who do good works. This we pray, in Jesus' name. Amen

Salvation

God made Jesus, who had no sin in Him, to become sin for us, so that in Jesus we might become the righteousness of God. It was His love. God so loved the world, that He gave His only begotten Son, that whosoever believes in Him should not perish, but have everlasting life.

Even Me

FATHER, in the name of Jesus, I thank you for the privilege to come boldly to your Throne of Grace. I come to amend my ways and my doings, so I can dwell with you in peace.

I believe Jesus died on the cross for my sins.
I believe through his shed blood, I receive forgiveness of my sins.
I believe Jesus was buried, and rose again on the third day.
I believe he is seated together with you, on your right hand.

Come into my heart Jesus, and forgive me of my sins. I believe you heard me and have forgiven me. Thank you Jesus, for your forgiveness. Thank you, for coming to live in my heart.

I wholly give my heart to you. I willingly depart from sin so the light of your glory can shine through my life.

Let the fire of your spirit, burn and purge the waste places in my heart. Father, I stand naked before you. If my heart condemns me, you are greater, and I must answer to you; so examine me. Search me, and know me. Reveal the hidden things of my heart, to me.

Your Word pierces and separates the soul and the spirit. It is a discerner of the thoughts and intents of my heart.

I pray you will let your light shine in the corners of my heart. Cause me to examine myself, and become totally committed to you. My desire above all else is to live with you eternally; and to escape, the wrath to come. In Jesus' name I pray, amen!

It's Time

FATHER, the harvest is past, the summer is ended, and some of our loved ones are still not saved. For this reason, we cannot hold our peace. Hear the cries of our hearts.

If our heads were waters and our eyes a fountain of tears, we would weep day and night for the lost. We would cry aloud and spare not. We would lift up our voice like a trumpet, sharing your love with the lost.

We have heard the 'sound of the trumpet'. The 'alarm of war' has gone forth. The end-time is upon us. Father, we seek your mercy!

We pray that you would wash, the wickedness out of the hearts of sinners that they might be saved.

Let none be lost O God, let none be lost. Let Calvary be remembered. Lead us back to the cross where Jesus died. Stir our hearts and minds to remember the work, which was done on Calvary. Let us bow our hearts and our knees to Jesus.

Father, we pray that the dark clouds of sin are removed from the heads of sinners. We pull down the scales of blindness from their eyes. We pray, with their hearts they will believe, and receive the salvation of our God. In the name of Jesus we pray, amen.

Stand in the Gap

FATHER, your Word is settled in heaven. It is a lamp unto our feet, and a light unto our path. We delight in your Word. Deal with us according to our faith in your Word. We hide your Word in our hearts that we might not sin against you.

Father, we thank you for our advocate, our mediator between God and man, which is the Lord Jesus Christ. Even as He makes intercession for us, let us make intercession for others. Give us a love for souls. Your Word says, "He who wins souls is wise", so let the spirit of wisdom rest upon us.

Encourage us to stand in the gap; to go into the highway and hedges, and tell the lost, you love them. Cause us to show your love to the sinner. With loving-kindness draw sinners to you. Show them, their transgressions and their sins, and help them turn from their wicked ways. We stand in the gap for those who are struggling, in the midst of their wilderness, whatever their wilderness might be. We destroy the dry places.

We decree and declare, we are moving forward. We decree and declare, we are not distracted by the sword of the enemy! We refuse to walk in fear. The fear of rejection will not prevent us from sharing your Word.

We thank you Lord for establishing us as a tower, and a fortress, in the midst of sinners. We decree that every sinner seeking answers will find you, and will not see another harvest, or another summer, having not committed their lives to you. Thank you for this victory, in Jesus' name. Amen!

I Surrender

FATHER, in the name of Jesus, I surrender myself to you. I surrender my spirit, soul and body, for you to use, as you desire. Teach me your ways. I have made a decision to follow you, and there is no turning back. My heart is fixed, and ready to move forward in you.

I decree and declare, I have placed my hands in yours, and I will not look back. I have counted the cost, and am willing to pay the price.

Father, I come to you, with a humble heart, and a bow down head. I come seeking your face. Seeking to know, what you require of me. My heart's desire is to obey your will.

Before you formed me in the belly, you knew me. You know me better than I know myself. Yet, you have accepted me as your child. You drew me to yourself, and made me yours. You have chosen to live in my heart. It is in you, that I live, move, and have my beings. I can do nothing without you.

Father, prepare me to fulfill your purpose, for my life. I will go where you send me. I will speak whatever you command me to speak. Place your words in my mouth, that I only speak what is pleasing to you. The earth is yours and everything in it; so all that I would give you, came from you. Here I am Lord, take all of me, and use me for your glory! In Jesus' name I pray. Amen.

I'm Available

FATHER, in the name of Jesus, teach us the true meaning of being available to you. Teach us, what it means to lay down our lives. Let us prostrate before you, and seek your face. Let our hearts and ears be open to your voice.

You are good, and your mercy is everlasting. You are the same, yesterday, today and forever.

Father, we pray that you would use us like you used:

Abraham, and made him a Father of many nations.
Like Jeremiah, who you called to be a Prophet, before he came forth out of the womb.
Use us like you used Moses, when the children of Israel were surrounded, with nowhere to turn, you made a way in the wilderness, and a path through the Red Sea.
Like Gideon, who defeated his enemies, by your wisdom, even when he didn't understand his position in you.
Use us like you used Jehoshaphat, when all the odds were against him, you won the victory for him, and he didn't even have to fight.
Like David, who slew the giant Goliath, and cut off his head, because he defied the only true and living God.

We thank you for using us. We give our life to you. Despite what comes our way, our eyes are upon you. We will trust your grace.

Whether old like Abraham, young like Jeremiah, educated like Moses, poor like Gideon, fearful like Jehoshaphat, or bold like David, we will trust your grace. You are the same God! You can do it again in our lives. In Jesus' name we pray, amen.

God Is with Me

FATHER, thank you, for being with me to deliver me. You have given me your strength, in my weakness. You have enabled me to break up my fallow ground. You have delivered me from my misconceptions and confusions. You are an all-sufficient God, and I thank you, for being with me.

I'm yours. I belong to you. All that I possess belongs to you.

You are my God, and in you, I put my trust. Let me not be ashamed.

Let not my enemies, triumph over me.

I will look to the hills from whence cometh my help. My help comes from thee, O God, the Maker of heaven and earth.

You will not suffer my feet to be moved.

You uphold me with your right hand, and there is no one who can pluck me out of your hand.

Your presence holds me steady, comforts me, and keeps me on your holy path.

You are God! You give power to the faint; and to them who have no might, you increase strength.

You are a powerful, and wonderful Father, who has chosen to dwell with me. You make me feel special. There is nobody, nowhere like you.

When I consider you, in all of your glory, I rejoice. I rejoice because of your love. You love me so much, and you promise to be with me always, even to the ends of the world.

I rejoice, because my name is written, in the Book of Life. You forgave my sins. I walk in your truth and I am sealed. I bear your mark in my body. I'm yours. In the name of Jesus, I say thank you, for being with me. Amen.

Casting My Cares

FATHER, you developed ways in my wilderness, which brought me deliverance. You have led me in a clear path. As I went step-by-step, you opened the way before me. Thank you for directing my footsteps.

I cast all of my cares upon you. I know you care for me. I am your workmanship, created in Christ Jesus unto good works. Before the foundation of the world, you ordained that I should walk in good works.

I cast my heart upon your Altar, and say use me Lord, for your service. Draw me nearer everyday. I am willing to run on, all of the way.

I fully commit all of the members of my body to you.

Let your Word be alive in my heart, and in my mouth.

You have made me a light in the world. Let my light shine before men, that they might glorify your name, in the earth.

I submit my will to you. Not my will O God, but thy will be done.

I want to hear you say, "Well-done thou good and faithful servant". I am living to hear you say, well done.

Despite my faults and failures, I will never let go of your hand. I will never turn back from following you. Father, make me worthy of your Kingdom. You alone can make me worthy, O God. I want to be acceptable for your use. I will press forward towards the mark, of the high calling in you. I cast my actions, reactions, and attitudes upon you.

You are the Potter. I am the clay. Make me and mold me into the vessel, you have called me to be. In Jesus' name, amen.

Carry Me

FATHER, you said in your Word, that even to my old age, you would carry me and bear me up. You promised that you alone would deliver me. You said that my deliverance was in you. These are your words, and until heaven and earth pass, not one jot of your Word will fail.

I decree and declare that your Word is fulfilled this day in my life. Let the full manifestation of your Word be present in my life from this day forward. No weapon formed against me shall prosper. All plots, plans, and strategies of the wicked one, are destroyed by the power of the blood of Jesus.

Father, you are a God who cannot lie. Whatsoever you have promised, you will perform it. You are not slack concerning your promises. You are a true and faithful God.

I rest on the promises of your Word. I do not lean to my own understanding. My hope is in you. In the good times, and the bad times, you have been with me. You have never failed me. Thank you, for your faithfulness.

I decree and declare, the glory of my latter house shall be greater than of the former; and I shall live in peace. Peace, which passes all understanding. Peace that the world has not known, and does not understand. I walk in your peace, as I go out and come in. Thank you, for your peace.

Father, in the name of Jesus, I ask you to revive the work of my hands. Use me to do new and mighty works. Let your glory be revealed.

In the magnitude of your mercy, remember me. I am known by your name. You are my light in darkness. You are my God, the faithful, the just, and THE LOVING. You cover and protect me from the evil in the world. You have brought me through the valleys and the shadows of death. I was not afraid, because you were with me. You are my praise. Thank you, for being my Father. In Jesus' name I pray, amen.

The Mind

This is such a critical area in the world today. Evil and distorted minds are committing crimes unimaginable. Good minds are under attack with dementia and Alzheimer's disease. We must cover our minds every minute of every day. We should speak only what God says about our mind. To do that, we must be mindful of His covenant with us, and to a thousand generations. He promised to keep us in perfect peace if we keep our mind on Him and trust Him to take care of us. Let us love God with all our heart, soul, and mind.

A Transformed Mind

FATHER, IN THE NAME OF JESUS I COME BEFORE YOUR THRONE. YOU SAID WE ARE TO HAVE THE mind of Christ. Your Word reveals the mind of Christ. I come that you might show me the specific things you require of me. I want to always be mindful of your covenant with me. I want to finish all that you have assigned for me to do.

I decree and declare, I have received your Word with all readiness of mind, and I have searched the scriptures for myself. Jesus, you know the mind of the Spirit, so search my heart and intercede for me according to the will of God.

Father, I thank you that my life is hid in Christ and I am not conformed to this world. My mind has been transformed and renewed. I decree, my life in Christ will manifest the good, acceptable, and perfect will of God. Holy Spirit, lead me in the way of God.

I decree and declare, I will walk after the Spirit and do the things of the spirit. I denounce the deeds of my flesh, and I do not fulfill the desires of my flesh. Father your Word says, to be carnally minded is death, but to be spiritually minded is life and peace. I choose life and peace.

You said, you would do a new thing in me and it shall spring forth. I command those new things to be manifested in my life now, in the name of Jesus. Father, you promised to make a way in my wilderness and rivers in my desert. I speak to the pathways of my life, and call forth clarity. Thank you that the former things are passed away and I walk in your newness of life.

I decree and declare, I am a new creation in Christ Jesus and my former life shall not hold me in bondage. My mind has been renewed. I will sing A NEW SONG, BECAUSE GOD HAS DONE MARVELOUS THINGS IN MY LIFE. HIS LOVE has given me the victory. It is in Jesus' name that I proclaim these truths, amen.

A Strong Mind

FATHER, I thank you for keeping my mind strong and stable. Thank you for keeping me in perfect peace, because my mind is stayed on you and my trust is in you. Your peace, which passes all understanding, has kept my heart and mind steadfast. I thank you for freeing my mind from spiteful and evil thoughts. Whether I am asleep or awake, your Word has transformed my mind to think your thoughts. Your thoughts give me hope.

Thank you that I have the mind of Christ. I am able to think clearly, soundly, and can actively do for myself. I love you with all my heart, soul, strength, and mind. My mind is not blind. The god of this world has not blinded my mind, because I believe the glorious gospel of Christ. I have been renewed in the spirit of my mind. You have not given me the spirit of fear, but of power, and of love, and of a sound mind.

My heart will not be lifted up, or my mind hardened in pride. I will serve you with all humility of mind. My tears and temptations will not change my mind. I will not look back. I am not double-minded or unstable. I will retain the knowledge of you in my heart, and will be persuaded by my own mind. I will remember Jesus, who endured the cross for me, lest I become wearied and faint in my mind.

Father, I thank you that to the pure all things are pure, but to those who are defiled and unbelieving nothing is pure. Father, I thank you that the memory of the just is blessed, and I am named among the just. I thank you for my supernatural memory and recall. In Jesus' name, amen.

A Oneness of Mind

FATHER, in the name of Jesus, we call to remembrance the work you have performed in the midst of your people. We will not set our minds on that which you have done, rather on that which you require of us.

We are commanded to serve you with a perfect heart and a willing mind. You reminded us that even though we are many members, we are one body. You said, "Fulfill ye my joy, that ye be likeminded, having the same love, being of one accord, of one mind."

Father, you require us to maintain a spirit of oneness, so we with one mind and one mouth may glorify you. Let us be one even as you and Jesus are one. Let us be perfectly joined together with the same mind and the same judgment. Let the unity of your spirit dwell within our hearts.

You search all hearts and understand all the imaginations of our thoughts. There is nothing hid from you. We come against any and everyone who would stir up confusion and division in the midst of your people, turning brethren against brethren. We bind the spirit of discord among the brethren.

Father, let us not walk in the vanity of our minds. Let us do nothing through strife or vainglory. Let us esteem others better than ourselves. Anoint us to walk in mercy, kindness, humility, meekness, and longsuffering.

Father, you have command us to be of the same mind one towards another. Mind not high things, be considerate to men of low estate, and be not wise in our own conceits. Let us be sober-minded, and not be deceived to think that gain is godliness.

I decree and declare, your people will be of one mind and live in peace, striving together for the faith of the Gospel, drawing closer to you. In Jesus' name, amen.

Mind Control

FATHER, we come humbly before you, committing the deepest recesses of our minds to you. You are our mind regulator. You are the answer to every question in our heart. You made provisions for us to protect and control our minds. Your Word is our antidote for every aspect of our mind. We thank you for our deliverance.

Your Word instructed us to think on things that are true, honest, just, pure, lovely, and of good report. We decree and declare, we will live and partake in that which is virtuous and praiseworthy. We will not entertain gossip, lies, or assumptions. We will not think on things, which do not edify you, the listener, or ourselves.

Father, keep our face like flint towards you. Let our thoughts be with purpose and praise. Fill our hearts and minds with your Word until it overflows. Give us a hunger and a thirst for your Word, that idle thoughts and communications will be an offense to us.

We decree and declare, we will meditate on your Word day and night, so what proceeds from our mouths will be excellent and praiseworthy. We will not assume the worst of others, but the best. We will not practice hurting others through our words.

Father, we repent of all our sinful thoughts and acts against others. We release them and pray for you to release us. We repent for any participation we've shared in damaging another's reputation. Forgive us now, we pray. We place a guard over our mouths, that we do not harm another with our words. We cover our ears so we won't receive negative things about others or ourselves.

We call forth the spirit of harmony into our spirits. We decree and declare we will dwell in peace and love. Our works will be in excellence unto you. Even as we respect you and your Word, we will respect one another. We will not defraud one another with our thoughts and words. In Jesus' name, amen.

Confessions of Faith

Years ago, a friend shared a list of "confessions" with me. Each confession had a Bible Scripture assigned to it. I used that information as a base, and further developed it to be used in our every day practical life. Let these confessions empower you, to walk into your destiny.

I AM the Apple of His Eye

FATHER, I come to say thank you. Thank you for making me the apple of your eye. YOU are the GREAT I AM. Thank you for transforming me into your image. Your image in me, allows others to see righteousness in the earth. Let my life show forth your countenance.

As the apple of your eye, I am special to you. You have protected me, from the plots and plans of the enemy. Thank you for the stability, and security I have in you. I make my confessions, based on the faith that you have given to me.

By faith, I confess that,

I am a **child of God** and the Spirit of God bears witness with my spirit.

I am a **new creation** in Christ Jesus; old things have passed away and now all things are new.

I am a **partaker** of God's divine nature, and I have escaped the corruption that is in this world.

I am a **child of God** and the Spirit of God leads and directs me.

I am an **heir of God** and a joint-heir with Jesus; therefore, I suffer with Him, that I might be glorified with Him.

I am an **heir** to the blessings of Abraham, according to the promise of God.

I am an **heir** of eternal life, in Christ Jesus.

I am more than a **conqueror,** through Christ who loves me.

I am an **overcomer** by the Blood of the Lamb, and the words that I speak. My life belongs to God.

I am a **laborer** together with God, and I manage the resources He gives me, with integrity.

I am the **righteousness** of God in Christ. Jesus was made sin for me on Calvary.

I am an **imitator of Jesus,** as I obey the Will of God, and follow Him as a little child.

I am a **lender** and not a borrower. God has opened His good treasure, unto me.

I am a **light** in the world. My light shines in darkness. Others see Christ in me.

I make these confessions, according to my belief in God, and in His Word.

I am who God says, I am!

Father, let your Word be manifested in my life I pray, in Jesus' name. Amen

I AM Complete in Him

FATHER, I come to you in the power of your Word. Your Word says, that I am complete in Christ Jesus, your son, who died on Calvary, for the sins of the whole world.

I am complete in Christ Jesus. He is the head of all principalities and powers. He is my Lord and Savior. Jesus Christ lives in my heart. He has sustained me. He has brought me into the fullness of your plan, for my life. I rejoice over the plan, you designed to bring me into my wealthy place. Thank you for equipping me to fulfill my purpose in life.

Thank you for my completeness. Thank you for enabling me to confess, that:

I am **redeemed** from the hand of the enemy.

I am **forgiven** through the shed blood of Jesus Christ.

I am **saved** by grace through faith, and it is a gift from God.

I am **justified** and I have peace with God, through my Lord and Savior, Jesus Christ.

I am **sanctified** in the name of Jesus, by the Spirit of God.

I am **redeemed** from the curse of the Law, because Jesus was made a curse for me.

I am **delivered** from the power of darkness, and I have been placed into the kingdom of God.

I am **led** by the Spirit of God, and as His child, I obey His voice.

I am **kept** in safety wherever I go, because God has given His angels charge over me to protect me.

I am **blessed** coming in, and blessed going out. Blessings are overtaking me.

I am **blessed** with all spiritual blessings in heavenly places, in Christ Jesus.

I am **healed** by the stripes that were put on Jesus' body, on the Cross.

I am **dead** to sin and alive unto righteousness, in Christ Jesus.

Therefore, I live, I move, and have my being, in Christ Jesus. Amen, it is so!

I AM Walking in Divine Favor

THE LORD is my shepherd; I shall not want. He maketh me to lie down in green pastures: he leadeth me beside the still waters. He restoreth my soul: he leadeth me in the paths of righteousness for his name's sake. Yea, though I walk through the valley of the shadow of death, I will fear no evil: for thou art with me; thy rod and thy staff they comfort me. Thou preparest a table before me in the presence of mine enemies: thou anointest my head with oil; my cup runneth over. Surely goodness and mercy shall follow me all the days of my life: and I will dwell in the house of the Lord forever.

I am **getting** all my needs met by Jesus Christ, according to His riches in glory.

I am **casting** all my cares upon Jesus, because He cares about me.

I am **being** strong in the Lord, and in the power of His might.

I am **doing** all things in excellence, through Christ who strengthens me.

I am **obeying** God's Commandments. He will elevate me and set me on high.

I am **exercising** my authority over the enemy. Nothing shall hurt or harm me.

I am **living** above all my situations, because the Lord has made me the head and not the tail.

I am **establishing** the Word of God in the earth, as I proclaim the Gospel to those I meet.

I am **binding and loosing** things on earth, that they might be bound and loosed in heaven. I use my keys to the Kingdom of Heaven to access my authority.

I am **overcoming** the devil daily, because greater is He in me, than he that is in the world.

I am **seeing** things that are temporary; therefore, I am not moved by what my natural eyes see. In my spirit I see the real, permanent, and eternal things, which cause me to rejoice.

I am **walking** each day by faith, and not by sight.

I am **pulling** down every stronghold, with my mighty weapons of warfare.

I am **casting** down vain imaginations, and bringing every thought in line with the Word of God.

I am **being** transformed by the renewing of my mind, so the good, acceptable, and perfect Will of God, might be revealed.

I am **blessing** the Lord at all times. I am continually praising His Holy Name.

I am **walking** in love and showing the same love, that Christ showed to me.

In the name of Jesus Christ of Nazareth, it is so!

I AM Living an Abundant Life

FATHER, I surrender myself wholly to you. You are a just and righteous judge. I trust you and know you will bring me to the expected end you have planned for me. You have designed a path for me, which is unique to me. No one else can fulfill my calling in life.

I patiently wait for you. I believe you see, you know, and you care. You are in control of my life. You alone hold the reigns to my heart. If you don't lead me, I won't succeed. I am in your care.

Father, place your arms around me and protect me from the evil of this world. I belong to you. I bear your mark in my body. I am identified with you. I am known by your name.

I believe, therefore, I speak:

I am your child and I **walk in your promises.**

I am an **available vessel** for you to use.

My life **reveals your glory.**

I am your servant and I **walk in your grace.**

I am living in my **wealthy place.**

My cup is **running over.**

I am **healthy.** No sickness, disease, or illness dwells in my body.

I am **debt-free.** All the chains of debt have been removed from my neck.

I have **sufficient wealth** for my future, the work of the ministry, and to help the needy.

I am **chosen and anointed** to fulfill your call on my life.

I am boldly **proclaiming the Word** of God.

I am **filled with the wisdom** of God.

I am **filled with the power and authority** of God.

I am **filled with the Holy Spirit** of God, and I operate righteously.

I am a **follower of Christ,** and I walk in the path, directed by God.

I am **victorious in all things.**

Everything **my hands do is abundantly blessed.**

My **mouth is filled with good things.**

I am filled with the love of God, **lacking nothing.**

I **walk upon my high places** on a daily basis.

I give God the glory, great things He has done! Amen.

Marriage

Marriage is honorable and the bed undefiled. A man shall leave his father and mother and be united to his wife, and the two will become one flesh. Two are better than one, because they have a good reward for their labor. If they fall, the one will lift up the other. When they lie down together, they shall be warm. And if someone prevails against one, the two shall stand together with God, knowing that a threefold cord is not easily broken. God will keep us together, if we want to be together.

Blessing the Marriage

FATHER GOD, in the mighty name of Jesus, we thank you for the union of marriage.

We thank you for giving us hope in a world of turmoil. Because of you, there is still joy and fulfillment in marriage. We invite your presence into every marriage. We celebrate marriage, and rejoice with great expectation. We speak prosperity into the life of every married couple.

You said, "Marriage is honorable, a man should leave his father and mother and cleave unto his wife, and the two shall become one flesh."

Let each couple be united even as Adam said, "This is bone of my bones, and flesh of my flesh."

Bless their life together. Make them one. Let the spirit of oneness prevail in the midst of their marriage. Let their lives merge smoothly.

Bless them to be patient and understanding with each other.

Allow the love in their hearts, to grow and blossom like the sunlight.

Let forgiveness dwell with them continually.

Let their communication with each other, strengthen their love.

We decree and declare they will not be divided.
They will not yield to temptation.
They will not practice sin.
Divorce will not infiltrate their marriage.
Secrets will not separate them.

We proclaim eternal victory in their life. Let divine wisdom, and revelation knowledge sustain them. We decree and declare, they will love you and each other with their whole heart. We pray they will do that which is right and good in your sight.

Let them nurture, and develop their love, using your Word as their foundation.

We pray that all remain well with them,
as they obey your instructions for their marriage.

Father, don't let them forget that you are the center and success of their marriage. Don't let them think they can make it without you.

Bless their going out and coming in.
Bless their dreams and visions.
Bless their seed and the fruit of their womb.
Bless their legacy.

Let blessings overtake them.
Bless and multiply the works of their hands.

We thank you for blessing them and making them whole. These things we ask in the name of Jesus Christ, our Lord and Savior. Amen!

Enlightenment 1

FATHER, in the name of Jesus, we ask you to save our marriages, save our families, and save our homes.

Wake us up! Shake us! Stir up our minds.

Cause us to remember that a house divided against itself cannot stand.

Cause us to remember, bitter and sweet waters should not come out of the same fountain.

Season our words. Heal our waters as it flows from heart to heart. Let peace reign.

Father, like never before, an awakening is needed in our marriages. Shake us, and stir us up!

Don't allow us to deceive ourselves. You told us, our words can kill and our words make alive.

Yet, on a daily basis, we devour each other with our words. We deceive ourselves in thinking we can attack each other with negative words today, and tomorrow speak of our undying love. This ought not be so with your children.

Father, free us from ourselves. We choose righteousness. We break the power of darkness and deception from our hearts and minds.

> We curse at the root:
>
> all of the put-downs,
> the harsh insults,
> the sharp words,

the lack of patience,
the lack of love,
unforgiveness,
rebellion,
retaliation,
the "what's the use" attitude,
reading things into what was said,
quick tempers, and,
misunderstandings.

We curse at the root, **ALL** of the habits and actions, which are enemies of our marriages. We cast them out now; and we proclaim that our marriages are healed, in the mighty name of Jesus, amen.

Enlightenment II

FATHER, we come to you on behalf of marriages everywhere; marriages which are aligned with your Word. Those marriages symbolizing the holy union, you ordained from the foundation of the world. The marriage you blessed and said, "Be fruitful and multiply."

We stand in the gap for marriages, asking you to rain down mercy and grace, in the midst thereof. We intercede on behalf of honorable marriages, asking you to make them even more enjoyable.

Father, even as you drew us with loving-kindness, let every spouse who has committed their life to you, be a beacon of light, for their spouse who does not know you, as their personal Savior.

Holy Spirit, minister to the cross-cultural, interracial, unequally yoked, and equally yoked marriages.

In the name of Jesus, we come against the enemy of our marriages:

we bind every one of his devices, and his darts,
we rebuke his strategies, plots, and plans,
we pull down his strongholds,
we cancel his contracts, and
we stop his mouth from accusing us.

We decree and declare these things bound, by the power of the name of Jesus, the blood of the Lamb, and the Word of God!

We decree and declare, our marriages are happy and fulfilled; in the name of Jesus, amen.

Communication

FATHER, we come to you in the precious name of our Lord and Savior, Jesus Christ.

We come boldly unto the Throne of Grace, to receive mercy and find grace to help, in the time of need.

We come to you on behalf of marriages everywhere, especially those who trust in you.

Hear our cry O God, and attend unto our prayer. We pray that you would heal, deliver, and set free, the communication in marriages.

> *Help those spouses who are ready to give up.*
> *Heal those who think there is no hope.*
> *Restore those who have already given up.*
> *And strengthen those who are still holding on.*

We believe you can and will deliver. You are God!

You are Jehovah Jireh, the God who is more than enough!

We invite you into our marriages. Abide with us, and take control of every situation.

We welcome your Word, as our standard to live by. Let your Word come alive, in the midst of our marriages.

Teach us to respect, and honor one another. Let our speech be filled with love.

Your Word declares, "It is better to dwell in a corner of the housetop, than with a brawling woman, in a big house." We decree and declare, wives will not be brawling women, but loving vessels.

Your Word also declares, "If a man doesn't provide for his own household, he hath denied the faith, and is worse than an infidel." We decree and declare husbands will provide for their families.

Father, we know you love us. You sacrificed your son for our sins. And you care so much about the prosperity of our marriages, that you gave specific instructions to the whole family.

To the children you said, "Children obey your parents.
Honor your father and mother." We thank you for obedient children.

To the fathers, "Fathers, provoke not your children to anger, but bring them up
in the nurture and admonition of the Lord."
Thank you for the love of a daddy.

To the husbands and wives you said, "Husbands love your wives. Wives submit
to your own husbands." Thank you for the household foundation.

Father, we decree and declare that every marriage is built on your foundation. In Jesus' name, amen.

Intimacy

FATHER, in the name of Jesus, there is no greater love than the love you have for us. You are our perfect teacher and example. Teach us to be like you.

Father, make us one in our marriages, as you ordained it to be from the beginning.

Let the spirit of Abigail rest upon wives, enabling them to love their husbands even when their actions are unlovable.

Let the spirit of Esther rest upon them, encouraging their husbands to freely give them their love.

Let the spirit of Deliah rest upon wives, so their husbands will find rest and comfort in their laps.

Let the spirit of David rest upon husbands, to be men after God's heart, leading his family.

Let the spirit of Jesus rest upon husbands, that they will love and give, whatever is needed to preserve their marriage.

Let the spirit of Elisha rest upon husbands, so they will discern the evil that is against their family, and destroy it at the root.

Father, we ask these things in the mighty name of Jesus, the name which is above all names. The one who is the same yesterday, today, and forever! We cast all of our cares upon you, because you care for us. You desire our marriages to be blessed, and we say thank you!

Thank you for loving us. AMEN.

Dedication

FATHER, in the name of Jesus, let the words of our mouths, and the meditation of our hearts, be acceptable in your sight. Let our words be pleasing to our spouse. Holy Spirit, let kind words, flow from our mouths.

We invite you, Holy Spirit, to arrest the lips, tongues, and mouths, of every husband and every wife. Let the sweet fragrance of the Holy Spirit of God come forth.

Father, resurrect marriages everywhere. We release sensuous words one to the other in marriage. We bind the desire, to stray or slip into sin. By the power of the Word of God, and the name that is above every name, we close every escape hatch, used in marriage. In the name of Jesus, we bind silent treatment, and isolation in marriages. We tear down the walls and partitions, which separate husbands and wives.

We bind wounded spirits.
>*We bind spirits that are easily offended.*
>>*We bind angry spirits.*
>>>*We release peace in the midst.*

Let trust prevail in the hearts of husbands and wives.

Let understanding be in the midst of them.

Let it be easy for them to say, "I apologize"; "I forgive you" and "I love you."

Let these statements be a part, of the foundation of every marriage.

Let us call those things that are not, as though they were.

Let us speak our great marriages, into existence.

Let our confession be: "My marriage is made in heaven. My marriage is like the relationship of Christ with the church. I love being married. I want to make my spouse happier than they've ever been. My spouse is my best friend. I enjoy and look forward to the time spent with my spouse."

We decree and declare, "It is so, in Jesus' name!" Amen.

Contention

FATHER, in the name of Jesus, we decree and declare, husbands and wives will walk together, hand-in-hand, and heart-to-heart. They will walk upon their high places, and take back what the enemy stole from them.

We rebuke and cast out the spirit of contention. We cast it out of our lives, out of our marriages, and out of our homes.

We release fulfillment, and joy within the walls, of our marriages.

Father, help us! Help husbands and wives control their tongues. Your Word says, "…the tongue is an unruly evil, that is full of deadly poison." It can kill and destroy our marriages, so we surrender our tongues to you. Take full control.

Put your Word in our hearts, so life can flow from our mouths. Let your Word come alive within us. Jeremiah said, "…thy Word was unto us, the joy and rejoicing of our hearts."

Touch our hearts. Give husbands and wives the desire to pray together. Give them a hunger to study your Word together. Reveal yourself in the midst of them. As they unite in prayer, and the study of your Word, let their emotions be healed.

We decree and declare, that as we obey your Word, we will minister to one another in love. You are the solution to all of our problems, and the answer, to all of our questions.

Let the light of your Word come alive, in the hearts of every husband and every wife. Let the knowledge that, "A soft answer turns away anger", rest in their hearts!

Let us be eager to listen to one another, and slow to speak.

Let us not judge, one another.

Let us not degrade, but encourage and build one another up.

Help us to keep our tongues from evil, and our lips from speaking negative things.

Stir up our pure minds. We will not allow our tongue to be an instrument that the devil uses against our marriage.

Let us fortify ourselves, by thinking the best about our spouses.

Cause every wife to realize that, "A wise woman builds her house, but a foolish woman plucks hers down."

Cause every husband to realize that, "The strong man protects his house from the thief." Let HUSBANDS be alert, knowing that the thief is always on the prowl. He is persistent, and patiently waiting to destroy what they have built together.

Holy Spirit, help the husband who won't talk, to open up and commune with his wife. Cause him to be sensitive to her needs. Touch him, that he will listen, and respond from his heart.

Help the wife who is talking too much, to develop a quiet spirit. Teach her not to speak everything that comes to her mind. Give her wisdom in her communications. Cause her to be soft towards her husband. Make her heart tender!

Father, help us to treat each other like the Kings and Queens, we are. We thank you for hearing and answering our prayers, in the name of Jesus, amen.

Unselfishness

FATHER, in the name of Jesus, we stand open and transparent before you. You see our hearts, and you know all about us. Since nothing is hidden from you, there is safety in revealing the issues of our hearts to you.

There is no other place we would rather be, than at your feet, feasting from your table. We come, that you might commune with us. We, married couples, need your help.

We willingly merged our two separate lives together in marriage.

We joyfully desire to become one, but O God, we need your help to make this work.

The struggles of living separate lives are tearing us apart. Help us Father.

Help us to get rid of, our selfish pride.
Help us deny our desire, to have things our way.
Help us place our spouses' desires above our own.
Help us embrace the knowledge and understanding, of becoming one.
Help us change from I, me, and mine; to us, we, and our.

Make us one!

Remove the scales of blindness from our eyes, so we can see our own selfishness.

We cast out the spirit of selfishness, from our marriages. We decree that the light of God, shines in and through our marriages; in Jesus' name, amen.

Men

The pillars of our homes, churches and communities are in ruin. Daily intercession is needed. A conspiracy is found among our pillars. The old men are dying, the young men are being killed, and the hearts of the surviving men face fears. Death has come into our windows, and we cry aloud for our wise men, our mighty men, and our men of valor. Let the Word of God be a lamp to their feet and a light to their path.

The Blessed Man

FATHER, we thank you for the man who fears you. Whose reverence for you causes him to walk in obedience to you. We pray for this blessed man. Let him be a blessing, all the days of his life.

We decree and declare he will eat the fruit of his labor. Blessings and honor shall be in his house.

His wife will be like a fruitful vine, within his house.
His children will be like olive branches, around his table.

We decree and declare, he shall see prosperity, all of the days of his life. He will live to see his children's children. His heart shall continually rejoice in you. We thank you for the blessed man. In Jesus' name we pray, amen.

Intercession for Men 1

FATHER, we come to you in the precious name of Jesus Christ, your son. The one you sacrificed, for the sins of the whole world. We come in the name by which all can be saved. We pray for men everywhere. We stand in the gap on their behalf. Help them Father! Deliver them from themselves. Deliver them by your hand! Restore them to you. Set them eternally free!

We Pray For:
Godly men ~ Bless them and let prosperity overtake them.
Good husbands ~ Let them rest in their wives' love.
Good fathers ~ Encourage them to become better fathers.

We Lift Up:
Divorced men ~ Help them maintain your standard.

Men sharing custody of children ~ Let them provide stability.
Men working to provide for their family ~ Let equity surround them.

Father, Help Those:
Men whose visions and dreams have died ~ Resurrect them.
Men who have lost their strength to go on ~ Build them up.
Men without Jobs ~ Let them realize their true value in you.
Men who were adopted ~ Let them accept it and move forward.
Men with no relationship with their fathers ~ Surround them with love.
Absentee fathers ~ Reunite the hearts of the father and child.

We Stand In The Gap For:
Men in prison, guilty and innocent ~ Let their dignity return.
Dead-beat dads ~ Give them a heart of integrity and love.
Men on drugs & in gangs ~ Release them & raise their self-esteem.

We ask these things in the name of Jesus Christ of Nazareth. Amen.

Intercession for Men II

FATHER, we come in the powerful name of Jesus, casting all of our cares upon you. We lift up men everywhere to you. We ask you to do a work among them, which cannot be denied.

We Pray For Healing Of:
Men with prostate cancer or any sickness ~ Heal and deliver.
Men who are practicing homosexuality ~ Return to their masculinity.
Men who have a lustful spirit ~ Set free and deliver from the flesh.
Men with mental health issues ~ Heal their Mind.
Men who are impotent ~ Provide sexual healing to their organs.

We Ask For Wisdom For:
Men who are in authority ~ Let justice rule in their hearts.
Men who are burdened with pride ~ Teach them humility.
Men with oversized egos ~ Draw them to follow Jesus' example.

We Pray For The Generations Of:
Boys who are being raised by their fathers ~ Be a good example.
Boys who have been and are being abused ~ Send deliverance.
Boys who are surrounded by all types of evil ~ Cover and set free.

We Lift Up Men Who Are:
Preachers, Politicians, Doctors, Lawyers, Janitors, Sports Figures, TV Stars, Movie Stars, Homeless, Laborers, men in all walks of life ~ Help them keep their eyes on you!

In Jesus' name, we pray. Amen!

Intercession for Men III

FATHER, we come in the wonderful name of Jesus. You are great, and greatly to be praised. Marvelous are thy works. We come to you on behalf of men everywhere. With loving-kindness, draw them to you. Let them praise you, from the north, south, east, and west.

We Pray For:
Men who are single ~ Help them maintain their purity.
Men who are in the ministry ~ Strengthen them to walk upright.
Men who are committed and faithful ~ Walk into their destiny.

We Lift Up:
Married men who are violating their vows ~ Cause them to repent.
Men fighting in the war ~ Cover them with the blood of Jesus.
Men facing racial injustices ~ Let the judgment of God prevail.

Father, Help Those:
Men who are the "only child" ~ Bring fulfillment to their hearts.
Men who are angry ~ Let forgiveness rest upon them.
Men who hate their parents ~ Massage their hearts & give release.
Men whose minds are tormented ~ Speak peace to them.
Men who have self-hatred ~ Let them experience your love.
Men who are weak ~ Make them strong and enable them to endure.

We Stand In The Gap For:
Men who are in bondage to alcohol ~ Let deliverance come.
Men who are gambling away their resources ~ Open their eyes.
Men who are killing one another ~ Teach them that life is precious.

We thank you. You are their life and the length of their days. We pray that the manifestation of your Word will be seen in their lives, in Jesus' name, amen.

Intercession for Men IV

FATHER, we thank you for the privilege of entering into your presence. We thank you for the opportunity, to stand in the gap for men everywhere. We thank you for the 'Calling', you have placed on their lives. We pray that you would encourage and strengthen them, for the path of life you have designed for each of them.

We Pray For The Healing Of:
Men who are discouraged ~ Send encouragement.
Men who are distrustful ~ Teach them who and how to trust.
Men who are depressed and oppressed ~ Give them perfect peace.
Men who are confused ~ Give them a clear mind.
Men who are overwhelmed ~ Teach them to take one day at a time.

We Ask For Wisdom For:
Men who are arrogant and hot tempered ~ Teach them tenderness.
Men who destroy their neighborhoods ~ Teach them wisdom.
Men who steal from others ~ Stop stealing and go to work.

We Cry For The Generations Of:
Boys who are exploited by adults ~Break the chains.
Boys yet to be born ~ Preserve and cover the womb.
Boys who are confused about their gender ~ Deliver Lord.

Father, seal your instructions in the heart of men everywhere.

Let love, joy, peace, longsuffering, gentleness, goodness, faith, meekness, and temperance be the lineage of the men we pray, in the name of Jesus, amen.

Women

There is a call out to the women. It is to the handmaidens of the Lord, those who stand in the gap, calling sinners to come Christ. Their eyes run down with tears and their hearts ache because of the devastation of the children of men. These are women who have given birth and those who have not, because the barren woman has more children than the wife. The Children she has birthed is in the spirit. The women must return to their wailing walls, breaking strongholds and helping to rebuild lives. Let us be women clothed with the sunshine of hope, sharing the good news of the Gospel.

The Virtuous Woman

FATHER, in the name of Jesus, we thank you for the virtuous woman. You have blessed her, and made her a blessing to others. Thank you that she shows your love and devotion, by helping others. We pray that you will strengthen her to continue living a pure life before you. We thank you that she is kind and tenderhearted.

Father, we thank you for the woman, who reverence you, and serve you with her whole heart. We thank you for the virtuous woman, who takes care of her household. She is not a busybody in other people's business. She works hard and is excellent in business. She seeks your will for her life. She depends on you to direct her.

We thank you, that you have blessed the virtuous woman above all women. She is blessed going out and coming in. You have blessed the fruit of her womb. You have given her wisdom beyond her years. You have energized her, and she redeems her time. Thank you for covering and protecting the virtuous woman.

Father, we thank you, that you have preserved the virtuous woman. You have made her the head and not the tail. She has received grace and favor in your sight. You have kept her from evil. The evil plots and plans of others had no effect on her, because you were with her.

Father, in this day and age, virtue is not valued as it should be. Bring us back to our borders; back to the old paths of our forefathers. Let morality, integrity, and purity be planted in our hearts. Let them come alive in us, to help us live a virtuous life. In Jesus' name we pray, amen.

It's a Calling

FATHER, we thank you, for the intercessors who stand in the gap for your people everywhere. Thank you for the heart of intercessors. They weep daily for the release of your people from bondage.

We pray that sensitivity in the hearts of your people would be stirred. We pray they would commune with you without wavering, and without sin.

Your Word said, call for the mourning, and cunning women. Let them make haste, and take up a wailing for lost souls. We pray for the areas, which the Prophet Jeremiah identified. We pray for:

Wayfaring men---men walking around in a daze
Brothers with lying tongues   Liars
Brothers that cannot be trusted
Brothers that are crooked in business dealings
Proud Brothers
Families surrounded by death
Children being killed
Young men killed in the streets—gangs
Gossipers
Adulterers
Strangers who are conniving, and deceivers
Neighbors who are slanderers
Men without jobs---no reaping of the harvest, and,
Idol worshippers

We bring them all before thee. Some with broken hearts, discouraged, and tired. Others are disappointed, suffering lack, and confused. Yet, you are able to deliver. Do it for your glory.

Thank you for the mourning, and cunning women. We pray your blessings on those who have answered your call; and have gone forth to do the work. Bless and anoint them now, we pray. Bless and anoint them. Bless the works of their hands.

Through the Blood of Jesus we were redeemed to stand in the gap, and to work in the fields, which are ripe for harvest.

We pray that mothers will teach their daughters to wail, and to stand in the gap. Draw the little children to you, and let no one stand in their way. Father, don't let anyone's life be a stumbling block to the lost. Let our prayers be acceptable to you, and let our sacrifices be sweet in your nostrils. In Jesus' name, amen!

For Good or For Evil

FATHER, we pray for the Women in Zion. We call forth the Handmaidens of the Lord. We speak strength into their spirits. Strength to do what God requires. We decree and declare mothers, daughters, and sisters will hear the call of God.

Father, your Spirit has said, "For Good or for Evil!" To us, women, it is for Good or for Evil! We can influence for good or for evil. Let us not walk after the imaginations of our own hearts. We guard our hearts against all evil.

Father, teach us that there are consequences to our actions, as well as, our inactions. We speak strength to the feeble. We lift up the weak, and encourage the doubtful.

Father, you have delivered us. You have refreshed us, and reactivated our faith. You have answered our prayers. If we refuse to obey your voice and walk in your counsel, we know that there are consequences.

Father, thank you for the examples you have given us, of the influence women have with men. Let us be wise and not misuse it. Open the eyes of the Women in Zion, and reveal your truths.

> **Solomon:** the WISE—wives turned his heart away from God
> **Samson:** the STRONG—brought down by a woman
> **Boaz**: the RICH—blessed by his wife
> **Barak:** the WEAK—delivered by a woman
> **Adam:** the INTELLECT—fell because of his wife
> **Nabel:** the FOOL—family was saved because of a wise wife
> **Ahab:** the HENPECKED—wife brought down his entire kingdom

We decree and declare, the Women in Zion will fulfill the call of God. They will intercede for the nations. In Jesus' name, amen!

Sisterhood

FATHER, I thank you for filling me with the power to love all of my sisters. I pray you cover my sisters with your love. Let purity, rest in my heart.

I decree and declare, my sisters will not defraud one another. They will cover each other, even as you cover us. They will not gossip about one another.

I decree and declare, I am a shield for my sisters, and I will intervene on their behalf against ungodly plots.

I forgive the sister who has wronged me. Father, make me a gift to the sisterhood. Bless me and I will be a blessing.

Father, I pray that my sisters maintain their virtue. Let us appreciate and celebrate each other. I give no place to envying and strife, in the midst of my sisters. I will preserve my spirit, soul, and body.

I decree and declare, I will not show disparity between my sisters, because we are one body. Let unity be in our midst.

Father, teach us to encourage one another by building up, and not tearing down. Your Word says, "A man that hath friends, must show himself friendly." I will show myself friendly at all times.

I decree and declare, I will not be pretentious with my sisters. I will rejoice with my sisters when they rejoice, and I will cry when they cry. These are choices and decisions that I have made.

I unite my heart with the hearts of my sisters. Father, I trust you to take us where we need to go. Thank you for directing my footsteps. In Jesus' name, I pray. Amen

Intercession for Women

FATHER, in the name of Jesus Christ of Nazareth, we come to you. We come seeking refuge and deliverance for women everywhere. We pray you would teach women to hear and obey your voice. Give them the strength to rise up and move forward in you. Cause them to diligently pursue your call for their lives. Let your spirit trouble those who are at ease, allowing time to slip away.

Father, we lift up women with broken hearts. We lift up those who have been wounded, and abandoned. We thank you for your promise to never leave or forsake us. Thank you for being a comfort to those who are troubled. We thank you for the solace we have in you.

Father, we pray you will draw women to you, who have been forsaken, and grieved in spirit. Massage the hearts of those young wives, who have been rejected. You are our Maker and our Redeemer. We pray that you would bring restoration to these women. Let their dwelling place be supernaturally enlarged. Father, remove all shame from their midst, and let their reproach be forgotten. Father, do a new thing in them as you propel them forth. Make them joyful women. Turn their mourning into joy. Give them beauty for ashes.

We pray for virgins. Keep them in your care. Place your arms around them and cover them. Prepare them for singlehood or marriage, as you desire. Fill them with godliness and contentment as you give them the desires of their hearts, according to your will. Father, don't let these women fall prey to the snares of the enemy.

Father, we lift up barren women and we ask you to bless their wombs. We also pray for the deliverance of women with vile affections for other women, that they be set free. We ask you to strengthen the praying women. Bless the married women, those who are bearing children, and guiding the house. Encourage them as the weaker vessel to be strong in your Word. In Jesus' name we pray, amen.

Children

The promises of God, in Him, are yea and amen! We cannot forget that the promises are to us, our children, and to all who are far off. They are to all whom the Lord our God will call. Our children are a reward to us from God. They are olive branches around our tables. They are precious despite the physical state they've placed themselves in. We must intercede for them.

Children of the Kingdom

OH LORD, OUR GOD! How excellent is your name in all the earth. We are the sheep of your pasture. We know your voice, and no other will we follow.

We come into your presence with thanksgiving and with praise.

We come boldly unto your throne of grace.

We come seeking 'grace and mercy' to help us, in our time of need.

We thank you for the access you have given to us. You have invited us to come. You said, "Whosoever will, let him come."

You have opened your arms and welcomed us. Your eyes have watched over us. Your ears have been opened to our cry. Even when backs were turned against us, you picked us up and comforted us.

Thanking you seems so insufficient at times, but we willingly offer our sacrifices of praise to you. With the fruit of our lips, we give you praise. Receive our praise and let it be sweet before you, acceptable in your sight.

Father we say thanks, thanks for all the things you have done for us.

For your goodness to us, we say thanks.

For your loving-kindness, we say thanks. Our hearts overflow with thankfulness.

Most of all, we thank you for the forgiveness of our sins. Thank you that you first loved us. Thank you for being our Father.

We are your children, in whose heart you dwell. We bear your mark in our bodies. We are identified with you. We are known by your name. We are free because you paid the ransom for us. We are the inheritance you so willingly redeemed. We belong to you.

Thank you for not withdrawing your hands from us. We need you. We can't live without you. You are our life and the length of our days. We are nothing without you. We are only complete when we dwell in you.

Oh Lord, our God! Remember us in our circumstances. Remember that we are the sheep of your pasture. You are our great shepherd. Our hope is in you, our trust is in you, and our eyes are upon you. We will look to you for all that we need. You are our sustainer. We look unto the hills from whence cometh our help, our help comes from you. You are our life. Father, this is our prayer, in Jesus' name, amen.

Deliver Our Legacy

FATHER, your Word says, "One generation curses their father and does not bless their mother. Another generation is pure in their own eyes, even though their sins prevail. Another generation is lofty and lifted up, being destroyed by their own pride. Yet, there is another generation that has teeth like swords and knives, which they use to consume the poor and needy."

In the name of Jesus, we come to you. You are the LORD our God. Heal us. Heal our land. Heal our children. Heal our grandchildren. Preserve us. Let deliverance come. Let the hope of salvation reign. Let the name of our God be known among the heathen. Bring forth healing.

We thank you for the grace that you have extended, to our children. Thank you for keeping them from lying down in shame and rising up in disgrace. Thank you for not allowing confusion to cover our children. Thank you that insecurity and instability did not overtake them. Thank you that the error of their ways did not destroy them.

Father, we pray for the future of our children. For they dwell in the midst of a mixed multitude of people, where right is wrong, and wrong is right. They dwell where evil is becoming more and more rampant than ever before. Sin has entered our land, and polluted the hearts of children everywhere. Every generation is at risk. We cover our children with the blood of Jesus; and we decree, they shall not be vulnerable.

Father, we depend on you to help our children. Destruction is all around. It was in our land, but now it has entered the homes. Don't let our children fall into darkness. We will weep and mourn at your feet, until deliverance comes. Just as Jesus kept all that you gave him, we decree and declare, that we will not lose any territory. We will lament until the hearts of our children turn completely back to you.

We pull down, every "seen and unseen" stronghold that is polluting our children. Father, let our sons grow up like trees planted by rivers of water. Strengthen them to become men who will glorify you. Let our daughters be like the decorated stones in your Temple, worshipping you with their spirit, soul, and body. Save our seed, we pray, in Jesus' name, amen.

Our Legacy's Creed

FATHER, we thank you that you are the head of the generation of the righteous. We confess this day, that our children are righteous. They have been taught your Word. They abide in your abundant peace. They abide under your wings. You are their shelter from the storm, and their protection from harm.

We decree and declare, the Will of God has priority in the lives of our children. They will cry aloud and spare not. They will lift up their voice like a trumpet. They will be heard declaring the Word of God. Their life will be an example for others to follow. They are trailblazers and followers of Christ.

We decree and declare, our children have hidden your Word in their hearts. They walk in obedience. Rebellion has no place in their hearts. They are the head, and not the tail. They are above, and not beneath. Our children belong to you. Take control of their life. Do with them whatsoever pleases you. You are their God!

Let our children lie at your feet, that they might know your heart, and obey your voice. We decree and declare, our children will not think that they are self-sufficient, but will put their trust in you. Our children will rejoice, because they know you.

We pray that fathers would teach their sons, and mothers teach their daughters. Teaching them your Law, so they will not learn the way of the heathen. We pray that the parents of future generations, will teach your Law even to the children, which shall be born. And the newborns shall rise up and declare the teachings to their children. We decree that they are mighty arrows in your hands.

Father deliver and preserve the generations of our children.

Thank you for hearing and answering our cry, on behalf of our children. In Jesus' name we pray. Amen!

Preserve Our Children

FATHER, in the name of Jesus, help us to love children, even as you love them. We stand in the gap for children everywhere.

You are an all-sufficient God. You are all powerful, all knowing, and you are everywhere at the same time.

Before you formed our children in the belly, you knew them; and before they came forth out of the womb, you called them to your purpose. We decree and declare, our children will go where you send them, and they will speak whatsoever you command.

We decree and declare, they shall surrender their whole spirit, soul and body, to you. We believe, therefore we speak: every member of their body is dedicated to you, and the purpose you have designed for them. They are completely at your disposal. Let your Word come alive in their hearts. Give them a love for your Word. Cause them to desire your Word, more than the necessities of this life. Anoint their lips, to speak your Word with power and authority.

Thank you for being with them. Thank you for delivering them in every situation. Thank you for being a faithful Father to them. Thank you for standing by those whose earthly father forsook them. You have always been present, to soothe the broken heart, and comfort the troubled soul. Thank you for being the "Head" of our children. In Jesus' name, amen.

Our Children's Declaration

FATHER, we commit our children totally to you. We decree and declare, our children will guard their ways and actions, knowing the consequences thereof. We speak to their spirits now and say, "Remember the Word of the Lord. Remember your teachings, for they are life and health to you."

We decree and declare, our children walk before you in righteousness. They have returned to the old path wherein they were taught. They are joyfully, returning to their borders. Let repentance come forth. Hear their cry, O Lord our God. Help us to walk in love, when dealing with our returning children.

We decree and declare, they shall repent and turn from sin. Father, receive them in your love. Give them the royal robe you have reserved for them.

Every time they sin against you, and return to you with their whole heart, hear their prayer. Maintain their cause. Perfect the things, which concern them. Remove the desire to sin from their hearts.

We decree and declare, our children are the light of the world. You have made them, a light in a world of darkness. You have called them and set them apart from the world. They are in the world, but are not governed by the world's system.

You have given them the strength, to obey your Word. You have anointed them, for a work in the earth. You have called them to pull down, to destroy, to plant, and to build. Our children belong to you. Do with them, that which pleases you. Give them the ability to know right from wrong, good from evil, holy from unholy, and clean from unclean. These things we pray, in the powerful name of Jesus. Amen!

My Legacy

I PRAY FOR MY LEGACY; my daughters, grandchildren, and the ones yet to be born; Le'Trisha, Jeanine, Kenneth Jr., Kristopher, Ashley, and Kaleb. I decree and declare, my legacy will glorify God.

Father, look upon Trisha, Jeanine, KJ, Kris, Ashley, and Kaleb, and bless them. Bring forth healing in their hearts, minds, and bodies. Let deliverance come to each of them who is facing struggles, or challenges.

Strengthen my Legacy, to stand as witnesses to the truth of your Word. Let their life be a testimony of their faith in you. I decree and declare, my legacy will trust you to lead them. Take full control of each of their lives. Let their lives honor your holy name.

Give Trisha, Jeanine, KJ, Kris, Ashley, and Kaleb, the spirit of wisdom, and revelation knowledge of you. Empower them to know you more intimately, than they have ever known you before. Keep them in the center of your will. Give them a hunger and thirst for righteousness.

My Legacy shall be a light in darkness. They shall be hope for the hopeless. They shall speak your Word with boldness.

I decree and declare, every generation of my Legacy will have a vision, and will run with it. They will not perish. Visions upon visions shall continually, burn in their spirits.

Their ears shall be keen to your voice. Their hearts shall be sensitive to your commands. Trisha, Jeanine, KJ, Kris, Ashley, and Kaleb, shall have hinds' feet to walk upon their high places. I decree and declare, they will not look to the left or the right, but they will keep their eyes steadfast on you. They shall love you with their whole heart, soul, and body. Their love for you shall be seen, in the life they live.

It is in the name of Jesus, I pray and believe you have heard me. And I believe I have received the petitions I have asked of you, because I asked in faith and according to your will. I say, amen, and let it be so, in Jesus' name!

Children and Electronics

FATHER, your Word says, "…and a little child shall lead them…"

Father, this world has progressed at a rapid speed. Man is leading himself to destruction. Everybody is right in their own eyes. Their wisdom to have more and do more has surpassed their knowledge and recognition of you. It seems you have become an after-thought; while their inner self, and even the universe, take precedence.

Father, you reign in our hearts. We submit to your will. You are our present help in the time of trouble. And we are in trouble. Man has become so educated and wise in his eyes, that you are deemed to have little or no value. You are being treated like you are just a vapor that has faded. Electronics have dominated the hearts and minds of mankind. There is no room for you. The sanctity of wholesomeness is being destroyed. Love, joy, and peace are not being experienced as in times passed. They have been removed from our midst, and replaced with the mighty electronic machines.

Father, our children have lost the art of oral and written communications. Expressing their emotions, and enjoying one another's companionship is fading.

We curse the spirit of death, which has come up into our windows. We cover every entry point into our homes with the Blood of Jesus. The spirit of death will not enter our homes, or cut off our children in the streets. Progression and advancement are good, but we must always watch and pray. Keep us awake! It is not the time to sleep. Advancement is subtle. It seems innocent, but can contain deadly poison. It doesn't happen quickly, but rather it is slow and deliberate. It will steal, kill, and destroy everything we've lived for, if we don't stand watch and guard our hearts. Progression is sanctioned by the majority, and provides a false sense of security, until it unexpectedly fails and hope collapses. Be with your children, O God, and preserve us from the enemy. In Jesus' name, amen.

What About the Children
(Template)

I PRAY FOR _____. I decree and declare, they will live a life, which glorifies God.

Father, we ask you to look upon them, and bless them. Bring forth healing in their hearts, minds, and body. Let deliverance come to each of them, who is facing any type of struggles or challenges.

Strengthen _____ to stand as witnesses to the truth of your Word.

Let their life be a testimony of their faith in you. I decree and declare, they will trust you to lead them. Take full control of each of their lives. Let their lives honor your holy name.

Give them the spirit of wisdom, and revelation knowledge of you. Empower them to know you more intimately, than they have ever known you before.

Keep them in the center of your will. Give them a hunger and a thirst, for righteousness.

_____shall be a light in darkness. They shall be hope for the hopeless. They shall speak your Word with boldness.

I decree and declare, they will run with the vision. They will not perish for the lack of a vision. Visions upon visions shall continually, burn in their spirits.

Their ears shall be keen to your voice. Their hearts shall be sensitive to your commands. They shall have hinds' feet, to walk upon their high places.

I decree and declare, they will not look to the left or the right, but they will keep their eyes steadfast on you. They shall love you, with their whole heart, soul and body. Their love for you shall be seen, in the life they live.

It is in the name of Jesus, I pray for _____ _____. I believe you have heard me. And I believe I have received the petitions I've asked of you, because I asked in faith and according to your will. I say, amen and let it be so, in Jesus' name!

These young men and young women shall come forth.

Thankfulness

Knowing what God has done for us and is still doing, we ought to live every day with a thankful heart. In this age of the "entitlement" mentality, we must ensure that our legacy is not swayed with this kind of thinking. Our blessings from God are tied to our thankfulness to Him. He requires thankfulness. His Word says, "In EVERY THING give thanks, for this is the will of God in Christ Jesus concerning you."

I Say Thanks

FATHER GOD, I thank you.
Jesus, I thank you.
Holy Spirit, I thank you.

Father, thanks for being God, in my life.
I am thankful that I am complete in you.
Thank you for the love, you have given to me.
You loved me enough, to send your Son to die for my sins.

I thank you Jesus, for coming to live in my heart.
I thank you Holy Spirit, for directing my footsteps.

Father I thank you, for blessing my going out and my coming in.
Thank you for perfecting the things, which concern me.
I thank you, for it is in you, that I live, move, and have my beings.

Thank you that I am debt-free through your wisdom.
Thank you for my health, healing, and deliverance.
Thank you that the blessings of the Lord have overtaken me.

Thank you for the unity in my marriage.
Thank you for the oneness in my home.
Thank you for patience and understanding in our midst.
Thank you for tender and forgiving hearts.

Thank you for holding back the hands of death.
Thank you for peace, trust, and strength for the day.
Thank you for the wisdom and guidance of my parents.

Thank you for the safety of my children and grandchildren.
Thank you for protecting the innocence of my children and GRANDCHILDREN.

Thank you for covering their hearts and minds in the classrooms.
Thank you for protection from the robbers, thieves, murderers, homosexuals, and rapists.

Thank you that my children and grandchildren are drawn to the right friends.

Thank you that abuse, addiction, and violence are not destroying my home.

Thank you that the spirit of suicide is dead, around me and mine.

Thank you that we stand completely whole, in you!

In the name of Jesus, amen.

Thanksgiving 1

FATHER, I come to give you thanks.

Thank you for redemption.
Thank you for salvation through the Blood of Jesus.
Thank you for a sure foundation.
Thank you for the indwelling of the Holy Spirit.
Thank you for being an all-sufficient God.

Thank you that my family and friends are saved, and filled with the Holy Spirit.
Thank you that my neighbors and enemies are saved, and filled with the Holy Spirit.
Thank you that the Nation's leaders hear and obey your voice.

Thank you that teen pregnancy has ceased to be among us.
Thank you for the fulfillment of single-hood.
Thank you for sanctification and holy living.
We thank you for the work you have begun, in the lives of your people
everywhere.

Thank you for all the missionaries, who have committed their lives to your work.
Thank you for being with them and sustaining them.
Thank you for their abundant provisions and traveling mercies.
Thank you for the refreshing of their spirit, soul, and body.

Thank you for allowing me to come boldly to your Throne of Grace, that I
might obtain mercy, and find grace to help me in my time of need.

Now, let the words of my mouth, and the meditation of my heart, be
acceptable in thy sight, O Lord, my strength, and my redeemer, in Jesus' name,
amen!

Thanksgiving 11

FATHER, I thank you for being God. Your name is excellent in all the earth. As the hart pants after the water brook, my soul pants after you. You have been our dwelling place in all generations. Before the mountains were brought forth, and before the earth and the world were formed, even from everlasting to everlasting, thou art God!

You are Alpha and Omega, the beginning and the ending, the first and the last. You made the heavens and the earth by your great power. There is nothing too hard for you. You said, "Let there be" and it was so. The worlds were framed and are held in place by your Word.

You alone reigns! You are great and greatly to be praised. There is none like you. Besides you, there is no other God. You are worthy to receive glory, honor, and power. You created all things for your pleasure, even us. With joy we draw from your fountain of life.

Thank you for your son, Jesus, the Lamb of God. Worthy is the Lamb that was slain to receive power, riches, wisdom, strength, honor, glory, and blessing. Thank you for the Lamb of God, which took away the sins of the world.

Father, we cry holy, holy, holy; Lord God Almighty, which was, and is, and is to come. Thank you for the love you have bestowed upon us that we should be called the sons of God. You are a shield for us. You are the glory and the lifter of our heads. We put our trust in you.

We will praise you with our whole heart. You are our rock, our fortress, and our deliverer. We lean totally on you. You are our Shepherd and we shall have no lack. You are our shield, the horn of our salvation, and our high tower.

Thank you for being our God and Father. In Jesus' name we pray, amen.

Blessings

FATHER, we thank you for Jesus, who came that we might have life, and have it more abundantly. We decree and declare, the enemy will not eat our harvest. He will not eat our bread or our flock. He will not eat our herd, or the fruits of our vines.

We are wonderfully blessed, and kept by your spirit. We decree that the enemy is defeated in our lives.

We decree and declare we have no lack. Our all-sufficiency is in you. You have covered and shielded us from the attacks of the enemy. Thank you for the standard that you have established, and the enemy cannot go beyond it. Thank you for your divine protection.

You are great, and greatly to be praised. You are God, and you are in control. You placed the sand as a boundary for the sea. The sea cannot prevail, or pass that boundary, unless you allow it. You are the one who said, "LET THERE BE" and it was so. You are God!

We belong to you. We are yours. You are in control of our lives. We are clothed in your righteousness, and kept by your power. Thank you Father, for blessing us. In Jesus' name we pray. Amen!

Bless the Lord 1

FATHER, I pray that men and women everywhere would praise you; lifting up holy hands and hearts, surrendering their wills to you. As they surrender to you, let a heart of praise come forth from their lips.

Let your people serve you O God; let your people serve you. Let us worship you. Let the nations bow down before you, because you alone are God.

You instructed the sun to rise and shine upon us; and the moon and stars to light our way in darkness.

You watched over us, all through the night. You protected us, from hurt, harm, and danger. You touched us with your finger of love, and allowed us to see another day. This is a day we have never seen before, and it is a day we will never see again. And with all of our heart we say thank you! Strengthen us to take full advantage of this day. Thank you for covering us with your compassion, and your loving-kindness.

Thank you for covering us with wisdom and strength. Thank you for your love.

We bless your holy name.
We bless you because you have enlarged our territory.

Bless the Lord our God, who has pleaded our cause, and has delivered us from those who lifted their hands against us.

Bless the Lord God who lives forever.

Bless the Rock of our salvation.

Bless the Lord God of Israel, who gave rest unto his people, according to all that he had promised. Not one word of his promise failed.

Lord Jesus, we are so grateful that you cannot fail, and you cannot lie.

Whatsoever you have promised, you will perform it. You are not slack concerning your promises. If you said it, you will do it. You are the same yesterday, today, and forever. Your record speaks for itself.

We bless you Lord Jesus. You have provided all that we need, according to your riches in glory. Amen.

Bless the Lord II

WE WILL BLESS YOU O GOD, AT ALL TIMES. Your praises shall continually be in our mouth. You gave us counsel when we lost our direction. You comforted us in our night seasons. You instructed us when we didn't know what to do. You have set our feet on a firm foundation. You have established us, in a secure and stable place.

We will bless and not curse. We will not forget your benefits to us.

We bless you for the voice of your Word, and the strength of your power.

We bless you for all of your works, and the dominion you gave to us.

O Lord our God, we bless you because you are great. You are clothed with honor and majesty. You are all together lovely.

We will lift our hands in the sanctuary and bless your name. We bless you, because wisdom and might belong to you; yet, you gave them to us.

We bless you because you have heard our supplications, and have not turned away our prayers. You have not removed your mercy from us. You have shown us kindness every day of our lives.

Every day you cover us with benefits, and give us strength and power.
Bless the Lord our God, even the Father of our Lord and Savior, Jesus Christ, the Father of mercies, and the God of all comfort. Bless your holy name.

Thank you for comforting us.
Thank you for being mindful of us, and visiting us.

Glory and honor, majesty and power, and all praise to your name.
We bless your glorious name forever and ever.

Let the whole earth be filled with your glory.

Let Zion bless thee all the days of her life.

Bless the Lord our God, who sends his angels
to deliver his servants that trust in Him.

Bless the Lord God, who has redeemed his people.

Bless our God, who hath blessed us with all spiritual blessings in heavenly places, in Christ; which according to his abundant mercy hath begotten us again, unto a lively hope, by the resurrection of Jesus Christ, from the dead. Amen.

Worship

When we come into His Presence, it should be with reverence. The Psalmist said, "Come, let us bow down in worship, let us kneel before the Lord our Maker; for he is our God and we are His people." We worship God simply because He is God.

A Prayer of Worship 1

FATHER, in the name of Jesus, we bow our hearts and our heads to you. There is no one like you. There is no one to be compared with you. You alone are God and we worship you. We honor you. We adore you.

We acknowledge you as the only true and living God. There is no one greater than you.

You brought the fountains and the floods together, and made them work as "one". You made summer, winter, spring, and fall; and you appointed a distinct time and season for each of them. You distinguished, the north from the south, and the east from the west. You provided the necessary food for the hungry soul, and water for those who were thirsty. You did all these things for our enjoyment.

The day is yours. The night is yours. You divided the light from the darkness. You prepared the light. You positioned the sun and the moon in their places. You designed the stars to shine in darkness. Yet, you are the light of the world.

Shine forth, O God, in thy glory, shine forth!

You established the borders of the earth. You situated them with the voice of your command. Saying, "Let there be", and it was so! No one can go beyond the borders you have set, unless you allow it. You are God, the great I AM. Besides you, there is no other god like you. We rest in you, now and forever more. AMEN!

A Prayer of Worship II

FATHER, we come to worship you. We worship your majesty! To Jesus, be all glory, honor, and power. Who was, is, and is to come; and is seated on the right hand of the Throne of God.

You are the King of kings, the Lord of lords, and the Prince of Peace.

You brought us salvation. You have loved us with an everlasting love. You have been with us from generation to generation.

You have fought battles and won victories for us. You conquered battles, which were too great for us. Even when we walked after the flesh, you dried up mighty rivers which would have overflowed us. You solved problems, which would have defeated us. And you clarified situations designed to distract us. You never left us alone. We didn't need to fight in our battles, because you fought for us!

When the enemy came against us, you lifted up a standard, which he could not go beyond. You crushed the head of the enemy. You trampled him under your feet. Then you gave us the power to keep him under our feet. For all of this we say, "Thank you". Thank you for being the God that you are.

Your eyes go back and forth in the earth. You behold the good and the evil; yet, you change not. You are still God. You are still our Father in heaven.

We worship your majesty. We willingly offer ourselves, wholly to you. Have your way in our lives. In Jesus' name we pray. Amen.

A Prayer of Worship III

BLESS THE LORD O my soul, and all that is within me. Bless his holy name.

Bless the Most High God, possessor of heaven and earth.

Bless the Lord God of Abraham, Isaac, and Jacob.

Bless the Lord our God, who has delivered us from the hands of our enemies.

Bless the Lord God, our Master Jehovah, who has not left us destitute; but has covered us, with his mercy and his truth.

Father, you are our Creator. Before the mountains were brought forth or the earth was formed, you were God from everlasting to everlasting.

When the earth was without form and void; and the heavens had no light, you made the earth by your power. You established the world, by your wisdom, and stretched out the heavens by your discretion.

You exercise loving-kindness, judgment, and righteousness in the earth, because you delight in them.

When you utter your voice:

> *the heavens speak,*
> *the mountains and the hills break forth into singing,*
> *the trees of the field, clap their hands,*
> *the vapors ascend from the earth,*
> *the winds blow, and,*
> *the lightning comes with the rain;*
> *all proclaiming that you are God. OUR GOD REIGNS!*

You are sovereign, and excellent in power. You can do whatever you desire. You live in truth, in judgment, and in righteousness. You are God, and we belong to you.

We are blessed to dwell in you. You are our life, and the length of our days. We glory in you. Our trust is in you.

We bless your glorious name forever and ever. In Jesus' name, we offer this worship to you. Amen!

Healing

Jesus went throughout Galilee, teaching in their synagogues, preaching the good news of the Gospel, and healing every disease and sickness among the people. That which He brought to the people is the same package He has given us access to, "The Completed Work of Calvary". He promised to restore our health and heal our wounds. He is the healer of our body, soul, and spirit.

Overcoming Sickness 1

FATHER, in the name of Jesus, we come to give you thanks. We come to worship and honor you. We come to lay our petitions at your feet. Thank you for granting us access into your presence.

There is none like you. You are great and mighty, in heaven and in earth. You are the true and living God! The everlasting King! The Prince of Peace!

We come on behalf of the sick and diseased. Your Word says we are healed. We will stand on your Word. If heaven and earth pass away, your Word will stand forever. We will believe your report even when things look contrary.

Father, you are the God who heals. You said you would take sickness away from the midst of us. And you said, if we diligently hearken to your voice, and do that which is right in your sight, you would not put any of the diseases of Egypt, upon us.

We stand on your promise. We come against all sicknesses and diseases right now, in the name of Jesus. We command the names and knees of every illness to bow to the name of Jesus. We cast you out by the authority of the name of Jesus.

We command whatsoever sicknesses, and whatsoever diseases there are, to dry up and die. We pull down their strongholds. We cancel all of their effects. We root up, and pull out, all of the residue. In the name of Jesus, it is done.

We speak life, health, healing, and deliverance, to every person's body that has been battling with sicknesses, and diseases of any kind.

We come against cancer, aides, alzheimer, dementia, high blood pressure, low blood pressure, diabetes, amnesia, long and short-term memory loss, heart disease, shingles, viruses, and all other spirits of sickness, and disease, known and unknown in the earth. We bind every one of them in the name of Jesus Christ of Nazareth. We trample them under our feet. We utterly destroy them, by the power of the blood, the Word, and the name of Jesus.

We decree and declare, a manifestation of healing and deliverance, from all these things, in the powerful name of Jesus. Amen.

Overcoming Sickness 11

FATHER, we thank you for access to your throne. We thank you for the grace and mercy, you have bestowed upon us. We come to you, because you are our life. We need you every day. We thank you for sustaining us.

The enemy has come to steal, kill, and destroy the health, of your children. We decree and declare, that he is defeated. We stop him now. We place our feet on his head. We deny him access, into our lives. He will not trespass on your property. We belong to you.

Jesus came that we might have life, and have it more abundantly. We shall not die, but live and declare your works. We shall live in divine health and healing.

Jesus was wounded for our transgressions, bruised for our iniquities, the chastisement of our peace was upon him, and with his stripes we are healed. He took our infirmities, and bore our sicknesses on the cross.

After the cross, he went about all the cities and villages, healing all manner of sicknesses and diseases among the people. Then he gave us that same power. We have the power to heal all manner of sicknesses, and diseases, through his name. I decree and declare, we will operate in the power given to us.

We believe that in Jesus, all things are possible. There is nothing too hard for him. He is the same yesterday, today, and forever. We call healing forth in the name of Jesus. Let manifested healing be witnessed in the earth, for the glory of God.

Father we thank you for the physicians, and the works of their hands, but we are calling on the great physician, the one who specializes in the needs of his people. We call on the name of Jesus. We speak strength to our flesh. We speak breath to our lungs. We speak clear sounds to our ears. We speak perfect sight to our eyes. We speak distinct smelling to our nostrils. We loose our tongues to speak with clarity. We speak a divine connection to our feet, legs, muscles, and bones, that they function as they were created to.

Father we thank you, that you are our Redeemer. You have redeemed us from the curse of sickness and disease. We acknowledge and receive, all you have obtained for us on the cross. We will maintain it here on this earth. We are the redeemed.

We speak healing, to the sick and the diseased. We receive our healing and we walk therein, to the glory of God, our Father. All these things we decree, in the name of our Lord and Savior, Jesus Christ. Amen. It is so!

Healing, The Children's Bread

FATHER, we come to you in the name of our Lord and Savior, Jesus Christ. We thank you for the living waters springing up in us. The waters that bring forth healing and deliverance.

Heal us O God, and we shall be healed. Save us, and we shall be saved. Our trust is in thee.

We decree and declare, by the stripes of Jesus we were healed. We walk in health, healing, and deliverance.

You are our healer and the health of our countenance.

Thank you for healing us, and healing our faith.

Thank you that healing is our inheritance. It is the children's bread.

You said when we serve you, you would bless our bread and our water.

Father, we know that you can manifest our healing immediately; yet, if you choose not to do so, we will rest in you. Our faith in you is firm. We accept your perfect will for us.

We thank you for healing our spirit, soul, and body, and making us whole.

We thank you for the peace that is with us today.

We thank you that there is no restraint for you to heal us. All that matters is, your name is glorified.

Hear our cry, and attend unto the prayers of your sons and daughters, who cry "Abba Father", day and night.

Perfect those things, which concern them. For Thine O Lord is the greatness, and the power, and the glory, and the victory, and the majesty: for all that is in the heaven and in the earth, is thine; thine is the kingdom, O Lord, and thou art exalted as head above all.

Father we thank you that everything, which rises up against us shall be condemned. We tread upon the head of all principalities, and powers. Our feet rest on the head of all the works of the enemy. He is defeated and we are victorious. In Jesus' name, amen.

Confessed Sins

FATHER, in the name of Jesus, we come. Some are weary, some wounded, some sad, and others are in bondage. We need to hear from you. We offer ourselves willingly to you.

Search us O God, and know our hearts. Try us, and know our thoughts. If there are any wicked ways in us, lead us into your way everlasting. You know our sitting down and our uprising. You even understand our thoughts before they enter into our minds.

Father you know the path we walk, the words we speak, where we lie down, and you are acquainted with all of our ways; yet, you love us. You love us with an everlasting love.

You have been with us from generation to generation. You have watched over us. You know our frame. You see our right and wrong doings. Where shall we go from your spirit? Where shall we flee from your presence? If we ascend up into heaven, you are there. If we make our bed in hell, behold, you are there. If we take the wings of the morning and dwell in the uttermost parts of the sea, even there, shall your hand lead us, and your right hand shall hold us up.

You created us. You know that we are nothing but dust, and our days are as grass. We are like the flowers of the field that flourish, and when the wind passes over, they are gone, but your mercy to us O God, is from everlasting to everlasting.

Father you have not dealt with us according to our sins; nor rewarded us according to our iniquities, but with loving-kindness you have drawn us to you. You gave Jesus as a sacrificial offering for our sins.

Thank you for your grace and mercy, so great is your mercy towards us. You have removed our transgressions from us, as far as the east is from the west.

Father, forgive us of all our sins. Cleanse us through the blood, and wash us through your Word. In the name of Jesus we pray. Amen.

The Breach

FATHER, in the name of Jesus Christ, your son, we come. We come lifting up heavy hearts and weary souls.

We stand in the gap for broken relationships, wounded spirits, and angry people.

Father we acknowledge the truth of your Word, which says: "It is harder to win back the love and trust of an offended brother, than it is to capture a fortified city." But Father, there is nothing too hard for you, so we bring our petition to you.

You are the source and power of our deliverances.

We come against hardheartedness. We stand in the gap for the offended ones, whose anger has shut others out. We stand in the gap for those who have been crushed, and are overwhelmed; and for those whose faith has been shaken. Their pain is perpetual and they don't think they can live through it. Father we bring them to you, because you care about them. You can deliver them from themselves. Their wounds have not healed, because of their anger and unforgiveness.

Day after day, they see the faces of those who offended them, those who betrayed them, and those who turned their backs on them. O Lord our God, cause them to release it, and let it go. Blind their eyes to the offense and help them to wholeheartedly forgive.

We decree and declare, that we are 'The repairers of the breach, and the restorers of paths to dwell in.'

We call forth the broken—you are healed and your wounds are bound up.
We speak to the waste places in your life—they are rebuilt and all is made new.
We decree that the breaches in your relationships—are repaired, restored, and renewed.
We call forth sinners to Christ—your heart will not return to a life of sin.

We decree and declare, the pains of the past are abolished and utterly destroyed, by the power of the blood of Jesus. We decree and declare, every person who has been plagued by a breach, is now covered by the love and presence of God. We decree and declare, they are developing a love for the Word of God. Their eyes are being open to the Word as a weapon for life. They are using their weapon to fight. The Word surrounds them with truth, righteousness, peace, faith, and salvation.

We declare these things to be so, in the name of our Lord and Savior, Jesus Christ. Amen.

My Healing Is in the Word

FATHER, in the name of Jesus Christ of Nazareth, I thank you for my healing. I thank you that Jesus was wounded for our transgressions, he was bruised for our iniquities: the chastisement of our peace was upon him; and with his stripes we are healed.

I thank you that Jesus bore our sins in his own body on the tree, so we could live unto righteousness. We were healed by the stripes he endured. The work was completed on Calvary. And we believe all things are possible to us.

Father we thank you for the examples, which you left on record to teach us what is good and right. Your Word says, "Jesus went around teaching and preaching the Gospel, and healing all manner of sickness and disease among the people." You sent your Word to heal them. They received your Word by faith, and their healing was manifested.

Thank you that our healing is in your Word. Our faith has met your Word, and your Word mixed with our faith has healed us. We walk in divine health. We have profited from your Word. Your Word has made us free. Your Word is life to everyone who finds it, and health to all their flesh.

Father, your Word is quick and powerful. It is sharper than any two-edged sword. Your Word pierces deep, and it even divides the soul, and spirit. Your Word is a discerner of the thoughts and intents of our heart.

When we walk faith and do not doubt, but believe those things we say shall come to pass, we shall have whatsoever we say. We can speak to the mountains in our lives, and command them to move and be cast into the sea. We shall have whatsoever things we desire, if we believe we received them, when we prayed.

Father, this is the confidence that we have in your Word. Your Word, which became flesh and walked among us, your only begotten Son, Jesus.

We know if we ask any thing according to his will, he hears us, and because we know he hears us, we know we have received the petitions we desired of him. His faithfulness reaches our faith and causes us to walk in divine health, healing, and deliverance.

Father God, nothing is impossible with you. I pray you would uphold me according to your Word that I may live, and not be ashamed of my hope. I decree and declare, the desires of the righteous shall be granted.

I bless you O Lord, my God. With all that is within me, I bless your holy name. I bless you for all of your benefits to me. You forgave all of my iniquities. You healed all of my diseases. You redeemed my life from destruction. You crowned me with loving-kindness and tender mercies. You satisfied my mouth with good things; so that my youth is renewed like the eagle.

Thank you for the healing power of your Word. In Jesus' name, I pray. Amen.

Prosperity

First and foremost, we must remember that it is God who gives us power to get wealth. We should not wear ourselves out trying to get rich, because prosperity is not in "money". The little that the righteous has is better than the wealth of many wicked. One handful with tranquility is better than two handfuls with toil and chasing after the wind. Let's keep our priorities straight.

Wealth

FATHER, we thank you for eyes that see, ears that hear, and hearts that believe. You have given us both the former and the latter rain, in our season. We decree this is our season. You have reserved an appointed time for each of us to receive our harvest.

By the authority given to us through the blood of Jesus, we call the north, south, east and west atmospheres, into obedience; as we speak to the wealth and riches of this world.

Wealth and riches, listen to our voices now. Whatever form you are in, bills, oil, coins, CDs, 401Ks, treasury, investments, land, airplanes, trains, cars, buses, inheritances, all types named and unnamed, we command you to come. Wealth and riches come to us now in the name of Jesus. Come to the Body of Christ now. You were stored up and kept in reserve for the just, so we command you in the name of our Lord Jesus Christ, come to us now.

We decree and declare, a supernatural transfer is occurring now across the nations. The hearts of sinners are seeking a child of God to bless.

And Father, when we have multiplied and increased, let us not forget that it was you. If it had not been for you on our side, the enemy would have consumed us.

We decree and declare, the people of God are debt-free, and we walk in the liberty of the Spirit of God. The yoke of bondage has been broken off of our lives, in the name of Jesus, amen.

War

FATHER, we come before you equipped to win, through Jesus Christ. We have on the whole armor of God, which enables us to stand against the wiles of the devil.

We take back all that the devil has stolen.

We take back every area of our health, our money, our parents, our marriages, our children, our homes, our churches, and our communities! We pursue, overtake, and recover all now, in the mighty name of Jesus.

Father, your Word is our medicine, and you are our great physician.

We thank you that we have recovered all.

We decree and declare, your blessings are overtaking the people of God, and we are rejoicing in you. There is no sorrow associated with your blessings.

We thank you for causing us to triumph in every situation. We walk in victory, all because of you.

Thank you that the creative power of your people is being manifested in the earth. Our creative power is coming forth in your strength.
We thank you that jobs, work, and careers are in abundance for the people of God.

Thank you for your loving-kindness, and tender mercies for this day.

Thank you that stress and worry have been destroyed in the life of the believer.

We decree and declare, the people of God are walking upon their high places.

We decree and declare, the believers are snatching sinners out of the mouth of hell.

We decree and declare, families are saved, united, and worshipping God together.

We thank you for the perils of life, which will cause many to turn their hearts to you, in the name of Jesus, amen.

Wealthy Place Confession 1

FATHER, in the name of Jesus, I call those things that are not, as though they were. I decree your blessings upon us. I release the spirit of prosperity into our midst. The blood of Jesus covers my mouth to guard and protect the blessings, you have preserved for me. My mouth will not speak both blessings and curses. I will say those things that you have said about me. I believe, therefore, I speak. I will not look to the left or to the right, but I will keep my eyes upon you. I will remember your promises to me. I will abide and rest in your Word.

I decree and declare that:

A godly foundation is being built in our homes and churches.

God is performing His Word in our lives.

The believers are walking in faith and victory, because the Word of God is being taught.

Godly ministries will reach the unreached, through the demonstration of God's Love.

I decree that the Anointing of God rests upon all believers.

I decree and declare, we will honor God by putting him first in our finances; giving him our best in tithes and offerings.

I thank you, Lord, for supplying all of our needs according to your riches in Glory. I thank you for granting us the desires of our hearts, and bringing us into our wealthy place, in the name of Jesus, amen.

Wealthy Place Confession II

FATHER in the name of Jesus, we thank you for opening the windows of heaven, and pouring out overflow blessings upon us.

Our storehouses are filled, so we can bless others and leave an inheritance to our love ones.

I declare an abundance of money is coming to the Body of Christ.

I call money to us, for the sake of the Gospel, and for our personal need.

I call our churches wealthy, with wealth in all positions, and coming from all directions.

I decree, parents are seeking Christian education for their children, because of its godly foundation.

I call forth finances to pay for the buildings, properties, equipment, and to do everything God has called the church to do.

I call our houses and personal properties "paid-in-full."

I decree renters in our churches, are becoming homeowners, as desired.

I decree and declare, we are wealthy and prosperous, and there is no lack in our midst.

I decree and declare, all resources which God provides to us, are disbursed with godly wisdom.

I believe we receive double in every area of our lives.

I believe we receive in a supernatural way,

> raises, bonuses, sales, commissions, contracts, purchases,
> favorable settlements, estates, inheritances, interests, income,
> rebates, returns, discounts, dividends, checks in the mail,
> gifts, surprises, lost money found, every blessing; we receive in a
> supernatural way.

We decree and declare, the believers' faith will increase as they witness the glory of God in miracles. These things we decree in the mighty name of Jesus. Amen.

Wealth and Riches 1

FATHER, in the name of Jesus, I bow my heart before your throne. You are the King of kings, and the Lord of lords. I am your servant, called by your name. I bear your mark in my body. My body belongs to you. It is the temple of the Holy Ghost.

I decree and declare, all that belong to me shall come to me! I am an appointed, and anointed, possessor of wealth and riches.

Father, your Word says, "Money answers all things"; and I need money. Not to love or hoard it, but to do your will in the earth. I long to fulfill my calling in you. Let your will be done in earth, as it is in heaven. I am available for you to accomplish your will through me.

You know all there is to know about me. You keep me on your mind. You assume the responsibility for me, and you seek to magnify me and enlarge my territory. All I need do is to obey you and follow your instructions.

Father, when I consider the things you have placed in my heart, I marvel; wondering, how will these things come to pass, since money is greatly needed!

If I keep my eyes on my situation, I would give up. Therefore, I will keep my eyes on you and the dreams you have given me. I will maintain my hope, and I will reach the destiny you have called me to.

I decree and declare, in the midst of all life's situations I will look to you, the one who holds the world in his hand. I set my eyes like flint towards you, the author and finisher of my faith. I keep your Word continually before me and I accept what you say about me in your Word.

You said, "The generation of the upright shall be blessed." I am named among the upright, so let your blessings rest upon my generation, and generations of generations, from now and forever more; in the name of Jesus, amen.

Wealth and Riches II

YOU ARE MY FATHER, the Creator of heaven and earth. The earth is yours, the world is yours, and everything in it. You hold the whole world in your hand. There is nothing hid from you.

You gave me light in darkness. You are gracious and full of compassion. Let your light shine forth, and let the glory of my God be revealed.

I decree and declare, wealth and riches shall be in my house continually. This is my legacy in the earth.

My faith is the substance of the things I hope for, and the evidence of the things my natural eyes can't see.
You made it clear that hope, which is seen, is not hope; for what a man sees, why does he yet hope for it?
I declare things that do not exist as if they do, because in you, they do exist.
Thank you that I walk by faith, and not by sight. Yet, I can see clearly! I see it in your Word, and I see it in my spirit!

I visualize it in my mind.
I prepare my heart for it.
I receive your promise concerning it!
I see wealth and riches walking to me.

Father, you allowed my enemies to ride over my head, but you took me through the fire, and through the waters; and you brought me out, into a wealthy place.

Thank you, for my wealthy place.

I decree and declare, my wealth and riches are manifested now; in the powerful name of Jesus. Amen.

Calling Forth Wealth 1

FATHER, in the name of Jesus, I thank you for the revelation knowledge you have imparted to me. I am wealthy beyond measure.

I decree and declare I see my wealthy place.

I live and walk in my wealthy place.

I honor you with righteousness, in my wealthy place.

I am filled with compassion in my wealthy place.

The wealth of the sinner has been laid up for me.

I receive the wealth that has been laid up for me.

I can handle wealth in the integrity of my heart.

I decree and declare, all that I am, and all I hope to be, are not in the wealth; but in Christ Jesus.

Thank you Father, your blessings make me rich, and you add no sorrow with it!

I am blessed in the city, and I am blessed in the field.

I am sustained by your spirit and I rest in thee.

I surrender to you, the wealth you have blessed me with; that your name may be glorified.

Father, you said in your Word, "Every person you gave riches and wealth to, you also gave them the power to eat thereof, to take their portion, and to rejoice in their labor; and all of this is the gift of God!" Thank you for my gift. Thank you that guilt and bondage have no place in the celebration of my gift.

I decree and declare, all of the blessings of the Lord shall come upon me and overtake me if I hearken unto his voice; in Jesus' name, amen.

Calling Forth Wealth II

FATHER, I come to you. You know my heart. Even though I need earthly things, my affections are on things above, and not the things on the earth. Help me to see myself, and my life through your eyes.

Let your will be done in and through me.

Let me keep moving forward, and not lose focus of the prize of the high calling, which is before me.

I will not be distracted by the sword of the enemy.
I will not walk in fear.
I will run this race in faith, seeing and doing it the way you would have me do it.

I decree and declare, the enemy will not eat my harvest. He is defeated in my life. Poverty, debt, and lack are destroyed from my life. My all sufficiency is in the Lord Jesus Christ.

Father you have covered me. Your truth has been my shield, and buckler.
You have established a level of protection around me, which the enemy cannot go beyond.
Thank you for seedtime and harvest. I thank you for the wisdom to sow seeds in good ground.

From the north, south, east and west, I speak to the wealth and riches of this world, and I say, come to me, come to me now. Come to me by the power of the name of Jesus, his shed blood, and the Word of God.

Wealth, I command you to invade and overtake the children of God.

We command a supernatural transfer of wealth and riches, to the people of God.

All of our debts are paid-in-full, and we are operating in the wisdom of God.

Now unto him, who is able to do, exceeding abundantly, above all, that we ask or think, according to the power that works in us, be all glory, dominion, power, and strength. In Jesus' name we pray, amen.

Tribulations

Whatever we are going through, we have the confidence of knowing that God is our hiding place. He is our refuge and strength, an ever- present help when we are in trouble. He will protect us from the storms of life. We will not fear even if the earth gives way and the mountains fall into the sea, because He is a sun and shield for those who walk with Him. Having this confidence, God works all things out for the good of those who love him and have been called to His purpose.

Preparing for Trouble

FATHER, I come before you, in the name that is above every name. The name of Jesus!

I pray you would give me a heart like yours. Condition my heart to please you above everything else. Give me a hunger and a thirst to know you. I want to know you in the power of your resurrection, and the fellowship of your sufferings, being made conformable unto your death.

I want to wholly love you, serve you, walk in your way, seek your face, and worship you. I come asking you to purge my heart, so I won't yield to the sins of my flesh.

In the name of Jesus, I decree and declare, joy will not depart from me, for the joy of the Lord is my strength. Despite what I am going through, the voice of gladness shall be in my mouth.

I will rejoice because I know my Redeemer lives. I will rejoice because I know in whom I believe. I will rejoice because I am absolutely convinced, he is able to do that which is beyond human imagination.

I am comforted in the knowledge of him and his love for me. I speak victory, joy, and gladness, into my spirit, because I know he reigns. I am not a victim; I am an overcomer in Christ Jesus.

Thank you Jesus for molding and equipping me to handle the things you have placed in my spirit. Thank you that I am unique. No one else can be me. I was designed to be me.

I am wonderfully and fearfully made. I am the apple of your eye. Thank you for me. Thank you for equipping me to do the things you have assigned to me. With you, all things are possible.

I move forward in your grace and mercy. My hands are blessed to accomplish my assignments. You have blessed me, and I will be a blessing. In Jesus' name, amen.

Suffering 1

FATHER, we come to you on behalf of those with heavy hearts, and weary souls. Pity us, O God; pity us! As your eyes go back and forth in all the earth, look on those who are facing trouble on every side. You see the gangs, the guns, the murders, the robberies, and the rapes. It is all before you. Look on those who are in the midst of these fiery trials and tribulations. And Father, listen to those who cry day and night, as their eyes run down with tears. These are they, who mourn continuously because they have lost their hope. Their souls are wearied and their hearts are faint.

Give ear O God; give ear to their cry. Hear the voice of their pain. They are in anguish and in need of you.

You are in control of everything necessary to meet our need! We put no confidence in our flesh, because it is not in us to direct our steps. Deliver us from ourselves.

Father we need you! You promised to be with us. You promised to direct our footsteps. We know you cannot lie. You cannot fail. And you do not go back on your promises. You promised to hear us when we cry, answer us before we call, and restore us if we stumble. Father, let your "grace and mercy" sustain us in this hour.

You told us to be strong, and of a good courage; and you would strengthen our hearts. We will not faint in the day of adversity. We will stand strong. We will stand in the gap for those suffering. We speak comfort to hurting hearts.

We decree and declare, no one shall let go of their trust in you. Even if they are at their breaking point, they shall not let go. They shall not look back. They shall hold onto their profession of faith. They shall not become weary in well doings. They will reap their harvest in their season. They will not faint.

They will know their God. They will know that your eyes are always upon them, and you neither slumber nor sleep.

You are our everlasting God, our Creator. Direct our lives according to your will and your plan. We will rest upon your Word. In Jesus' name, amen.

Suffering II

FATHER, we know that you chasten those you love. And no chastening seems good, but afterwards it yields the peaceable fruit of righteousness. We will wait on you. We will keep our eyes focus on you. We will let nothing slip. We know you have a plan and a purpose in our sufferings.

We will wait on you until our strength is renewed. We will wait,

until we mount up with wings as eagles,
until we start running and shaking off weariness,
until we begin to walk securely in you,

knowing that you watch over your Word to perform it.

Our afflictions have brought us closer to you. They have pushed us into your arms of safety. We will abide in you, and let your Word abide in us.

Before we were afflicted, we did things our way, but suffering has taught us to stand on your Word. It is good that our flesh was afflicted, so our spirits would develop and grow in truth and grace.

Let peace and truth be with us all the days of our lives, and let quietness be our strength.

Many days our hearts ached with pain, but for thy name's sake, we held our peace. We were determined not to speak contrary to your Word. Thank you for calling and preparing us for your eternal glory. You said, "After we have suffered a while, you will make us perfect. You will establish, strengthen, and settle us."

Father we thank you that no weapon formed against us shall prosper. Our enemies shall fight against us, but they shall not prevail.

You are with us to deliver us, and there is no failure in you. Suffering has taught us that our best strategy is to run to you. It is in our best interest to stay close to you. You have the Words of Life! You are our life!

It is in you, that we live, move, and have the activities of our limbs. We are more than conquerors through you, who love us. Thank you for our deliverance. In Jesus' name we pray. Amen.

Perseverance 1

FATHER, you are the God of our youth, and the God in our old age. We acknowledge our sins, iniquities, transgressions, and our secret faults before you.

We will not allow our iniquities to turn away your blessings. We will not allow our sins to cause good things to be withheld from us. We repent now, in the mighty name of our Lord and Savior, Jesus Christ. We bow our hearts and heads before you. We know that you are the only true and living God. You alone rule in all the earth!

Father just as you brought Israel out of Egypt, led them through the wilderness with a pillar of cloud by day, and gave them light in darkness with a pillar of fire; you can do the same thing for us. We need you to lead us and give light to our pathway.

Just as you carried Israel through the midst of the Red Sea on dry land, and watched over them through droughts, and the shadows of death, you can do the same thing for us. We need you to fortify our walk with you, until our hearts are fixed on you, and our steps are unmovable. Despite what comes against us, let us say, "The will of the Lord be done." We believe you desire the best for us. And you delight to show yourself strong on our behalf.

You are:
our water when we are thirsty,
our light in darkness,
our shelter in the storm,
our bridge over troubled waters,
our food when we are hungry,
our clothes when we are naked,
you are the health of our bones, and,
you are the Lord that heals us.

Our all sufficiency is in thee! You are all we need.

Thank you Jesus for your provisions. Your provisions shall be seen in my life. Amen.

Perseverance II

FATHER, we thank you for being a merciful God. You have shown us mercy according to your loving-kindness. Thank you for the grace we do not deserve, and for the mercy that holds back the punishment we do deserve. Enlarge our hearts to love you more.

Father help us to remember the work completed at Calvary. Don't let us forget the price paid to redeem us. We will lift our eyes unto the hills, where our help comes from. Our help comes from Jesus, the sacrificial Lamb of God. We dedicate our life to him.

Strengthen us according to your Word. We decree and declare, when we are strengthened, we will walk in your liberty, and speak of you among the heathens. We will not be ashamed.

You are our comfort in the midst of our afflictions. When we remember your Word and your promises, we are comforted. You have given us songs in the night. There is no God like you. You are our portion. Our trust is in thee.

As the hart pants for the waters, our souls long for thee. We desire your favor. Wake us! Stir up our minds and cause us to remember your faithfulness. Even in our midnight when it is the darkest, we will give you thanks. You are good and you do all things well.

You are more valuable to us than silver and gold. You have made and fashioned us with your own hands. Father we thank you that we are fearfully and wonderfully made; and marvelous are your works. Let goodness and mercy follow us all the days of our lives. Your will, O God, is our delight. We will never forget your Word. Through your Word you have walked with us. You have delivered us. You have brought us through difficult situations, time after time. Even when we thought we were at our end, your Word kept us. We belong to you. We will always remember that it is your Word, which will save us. We will keep Calvary, the shed blood, the suffering, and the completed work, continually before us.

You broke the yoke of the enemy and destroyed his hold on our lives. You freed us from the bondage of sin. You have planted us as a noble vine and a right seed. We are like trees planted by rivers of water. We bring forth fruit in our season. Our leaf will not wither and whatsoever we do shall prosper.
In the name of Jesus, we pray!
AMEN!

Yet 1

LORD, I promised you that I would hold on until the end. During this hour, O God, I need a Word from you. Speak to me and I will hear, and listen to your Words. My heart is turned towards you. I will obey your voice.

Father, revive the work of your hands, for I am the work of your hands. Revive me!

I don't always understand your ways, but I know that whatever you allow, it is what's best for me.

Teach me to take my eyes off of myself, and see Jesus. Let me see his glory in the heavens. Let me bring forth his praises in the earth.

For your brightness is greater than the noonday light, and your power is without measure.

Your ways are from everlasting to everlasting, in afflictions and in victories. You are God! You are my God!

When the enemy plotted and planned my demise, my belly trembled and my lips quivered, BUT THEN, I remembered your Words to me.

I ran to you to find rest in the day of trouble.
I stayed under your shadow and rested.
I was strengthened as I abode with you.

You loved me and cared for me. You washed my wounds and healed me.

You, O God, saved me from my enemies, and you even saved me from myself. I praise you O God according to your righteousness!
In Jesus' name, amen.

Yet 11

FATHER, thank you for the salvation I received through the shed blood of Jesus. I was saved from sin and destruction.

My enemies cannot destroy me. They cannot defeat me.

They came to eat up my flesh, to scatter me like a whirlwind, and to secretly devour me. BUT THOU O Lord has been a shield for me, the glory and the lifter of my head.

You are my defense. You promised to save the upright in heart. Save now, Lord I pray!

You judge the righteous and are angry with the wicked every day. You have set your arrows against my persecutors.

I decree and declare, my persecutors have made a pit and dug it, and they are fallen into the ditch, which they made for me.

I decree it! I declare it! It is so!

Their mischief shall return upon their own heads, and their violence shall dwell in the midst of their own houses.

I will sing praises to the name of the LORD, Most High.

For he has promised and he will come through! There is no variableness, neither shadow of turning with him. He is consistent and perfect in all his ways.

Although

the fig tree shall not blossom,

neither shall fruit be in the vines;

the labor of the olive shall fail,

and the fields shall yield no meat;

the flock shall be cut off from the fold,

and there shall be no herd in the stalls;

YET,

I will rejoice in the LORD, I will joy in the God of my salvation.

The LORD God is my strength. He will make my feet like hinds' feet. He will make me to walk upon mine high places. In Jesus' name, it is so, amen!

Authority

God is God forever, and He will guide us from the cradle to the grave. However, we must trust Him with all of our heart, and lean not unto our own understanding. We are to acknowledge Him in all of our ways, and He will direct our paths. If we look to ourselves for directions, we will surely be misguided, so even when we make plans, we must remain open for God to show us how to carry out His plans. All that we do should begin and end with God.

A Prayer for Clergy

Our God and Father in Heaven, we pray for clergy in general, and Pastors in particular, men and women who have committed their lives to serving and ministering to your people.

These are times when Pastors are becoming discouraged, disappointed, and frustrated. As a result, many are walking away from ministry.

When your servant David became discouraged, your Word declares, 'But David encouraged himself in the Lord, his God.'

You are the Father of mercies, and the God of all comfort. We ask you to encourage, strengthen, and comfort all clergy, who are struggling with challenges in ministry. Encourage them and lift them up. Remind them that you have begun a good work in them, and you will continue doing it until the day of Jesus Christ.

We pray O God, you would grant unto your servants boldness to proclaim the complete Word of God, in this day of compromise.

Father, as your servants equip your children to walk with you, we ask that you bless them to grow in grace, and in the knowledge of you.

Your Word says, "Study to show thyself approved unto God. A workman that needs not to be ashamed, rightly dividing the Word of Truth." This admonition is for your children as well as Pastors, because they cannot feed the flock if they are empty.

O God, we declare that no weapon formed against your servants, Pastors, and clergy shall prosper.

Cause clergy everywhere to be strong in you, and in the power of your might.

We pray that your Pastors will resist the enemy. For your Word declares, 'Resist the devil, and he will flee from you.'

Our churches are being challenged on issues relating to biblical truth. When they are challenged cause them to stand on the Word of God.

As they walk with you,

bless their homes
protect their health
save their children
touch their finances
encourage their spouses
unite their families
strengthen their marriages
protect their reputations
increase their anointing
fill them with your spirit
cover them in the blood of Jesus Christ
cause them to be morally upright
cause their faith to be unshakeable
cause their resolve to be unchangeable
cause them to be examples of holiness
when tempted, cause them to take the escape route
when they need to be restored, cause them to quickly run to you
cause them to walk in faith
let them be filled with hope
allow them to be motivated by love

Cause them not to compare their ministries with others.

Cause them to seek counseling when they need it.

Cause them to be people of fidelity, honesty, and integrity.

We pray in the name of the Lord Jesus Christ. Amen.

Jerusalem

FATHER, in the name of Jesus, we pray for the peace of Jerusalem. Let them sing with gladness, and shout among the nations. Father, save your people, the remnant of Israel. Bring them from the north and gather them from the coasts of the earth.

You promised to lead them, and cause them to walk by the rivers of waters in a straight way, and they shall not stumble. Though you scattered Israel, you promised to gather them back, and keep them as a shepherd does his flock.

You will redeem your people, and ransom them from the hand of those who are stronger than they. They shall come and sing in the height of Zion, and shall speak of the goodness of the Lord. Their souls shall be as a watered garden, and there shall be no more sorrow.

You will bless them with justice, in the mountain of your holiness. As you watched over them in their destruction and affliction, you promised to watch over them in their rebuilding and planting. Father, watch over your Word and perform it. Make Jerusalem a strong nation once again.

Make a new covenant with the house of Israel, and with the house of Judah. Place your Law in their inward parts, and write it in their hearts. They are your people and you are their God. Forgive their iniquities and forget their sins. They shall all know you, from the least of them unto the greatest of them. Let Jerusalem rejoice to the glory of God. In Jesus' name we pray, amen.

Our Nation

FATHER, you are the one who gives the sun to light the day, and the moon and stars to light the night. And it is you, who divides the sea when the waves roar. Your creation is so vast that the heavens above cannot be measured, and the foundations of the earth cannot be entirely searched. Man is but dust, yet, you gave him dominion in the earth.

This world is in trouble. Our nation is sinking deeper and deeper into sin. The standard of living is inverted. What is right is viewed as wrong, and what is wrong is accepted as right. Just as you judged Sodom and Gomorrah, we know that you will judge this world. Preserve the righteous, O God, preserve us from your wrath to come.

Greed has destroyed, lack of integrity has weakened, and the selfishness of the wealthy has consumed the poor. Hear our cry O God; hear our cry! Our only hope is in you.

We pull down the stronghold of greed in our land.

The wicked has become great and their deeds are overlooked. They judge not the cause of the fatherless, or the rights of the needy. They are like raving wolves.

We bind all of their evil and wicked intentions, plots, and plans. We decree that they are stopped, broken, and destroyed.

We decree and declare that our nation is returning to God, the true and living God.

We decree and declare that our nation is returning to the Word of God.

We pray for the United States Congress, Senate, and House of Representatives, who make the laws governing our country. We pray for the President, Vice President, and the Cabinet, who carry out the laws governing our country. And we pray for the Supreme Court and other Federal Courts, who evaluates the laws governing our country.

Father, direct the paths and footsteps of all in authority. Give them wisdom and strength to do the right things. Give them insight to know how to proceed and when to stop. Speak to them and if they refuse to hear your voice, speak to them in their sleep. Seal your instructions in their hearts and minds. Cause your spirit of conviction to rest upon all in authority. Give those in authority a heart for all people regardless of their race, creed, or color. Deliver us from ourselves. Forgive us of our sins. Let your mercy and grace be in our midst. In Jesus' name we pray, amen.

Our Economy

FATHER, your Word says, "Man born of a woman is of a few days and full of trouble." There is indeed trouble in our land. We need you to help us. Help your children.

In this economic crisis, the hearts of many are failing. They fear what tomorrow will bring. Lord Jesus, I am grateful to know that you hold my tomorrow. Many have lost hope, and are choosing death rather than life. Suicide and mercy killings are becoming acceptable. Life has lost its value in the heart of man. Murder is becoming the norm. In the name of Jesus, I bind the spirit of suicide, murder and homosexuality, which are rampant in the earth. I cast off the scales that have blinded the hearts of so many. Today, everybody is right in their own eyes. I reverse the curse that causes a lie to be accepted over the truth. I bind the spirit of deception that is in operation. I break and destroy racial and economic barriers.

We decree and declare that the plagues and moral sickness of our nation will be destroyed, as sin is revealed and repentance comes forth.

I break the yoke and cast down the spirit of adultery, fornication, uncleanness, lasciviousness, idolatry, witchcraft, hatred, variance, emulations, wrath, strife, seditions, heresies, envyings, murders, drunkenness, revellings, and the like, by the power of the Word of God, the blood of the Lamb, and the name of Jesus.

Father, draw our Nation back to you. Turn our hearts back to you. Let us return to "In God We Trust" and live accordingly. In Jesus' name we pray, amen.

In God We Trust

FATHER, our nation has chosen to reject you, your presence, and your Word. There is no hope outside of you. The deception of many is leading the hearts of the innocent and ignorant away from you.

The cries of our nation are answered with solutions that will take our nation to hell. Father we need a Holy Ghost intervention. Let revival break forth in the midst of your people. Let your people rise up and take a stand. Let your people humble themselves, pray and seek your face, so that you will answer from heaven, as you promised.

We know that your Word is forever settled in heaven. Your faithfulness is extended to all generations. We will continue to stand on your Word as we move forward, because your faithfulness is sustaining us. We will tell everyone that will listen, and future generations about the faithfulness of our God.

Let us live with a clean conscious towards you and all men. Let not the blood of the poor and the innocent be upon our hands. Don't allow greed to possess our souls. We give you our heart so that it will remain pure. Father, send your showers of blessings upon us. Let your latter rain fall on us.

Let your tender mercies follow us, that we may live a quiet and peaceable life.

We will perish in our afflictions, if we exclude you from our lives. The darkness of this world would cover us. We thank you for giving your angels charge over us, to guard and protect us from the wicked one, and the wickedness of this world. You have made us more than conquerors. We are victors and winners because we delight ourselves in your Word.

Your power is without measure. This nation can't fight with you and win. Open the eyes of those in Authority. Reveal yourself to them and cause repentance to come forth.

Father, even in the midst of your wrath, remember mercy and extend grace to your children. Cause those who do not regard your Word, to come and bow down at your feet. Cause the heathens to confess with their mouths that you are God! These things we ask in Jesus' name, amen.

Our Only Hope

FATHER, we come into your presence. You are the answer to all of our questions, and the solution to all of our problems. Who can contend with thee? Who is your equal? You alone are God!

When you speak, the earth tremble. In your presence, the mountains scatter and the hills bow down. In your presence, the winds run before thee, and the sun and moon stand still. In your presence, the stars and the clouds dance before you; and the Angels cry, holy, holy, holy!

All creation proclaims you to be God, while man fights to prove your non-existence. The Angels asked, "What is man that you are mindful of him?" They don't understand the love you have for man. Yet, man in his sins keeps moving farther and farther away from you. You are the same, yesterday, today and forever.

Your hand is not shortened that it cannot save. Neither is your ear heavy that it cannot hear. It is our iniquities that have separated us from you. Our sins have hidden your face from us. You cannot look upon sin. Our nation has made mockery of your Word. You will laugh when calamity comes upon our land, and you will not hear their cries.

So many of our leaders' hands are defiled with blood. Their fingers are filled with iniquity. Their lips freely release lies and their tongue is perverse. Their works are works of iniquity and acts of violence. Their feet run to evil, and they make haste to shed innocent blood. Their thoughts are thoughts of iniquity. Waste and destruction are in their paths. They do not choose the way of peace. There is no right judgment in their goings. They have made crooked paths, devising the destruction of others.

Father, let justice overtake us. We look to you for light. Darkness is covering our nation. People are stumbling in the noonday as if it were night.

We need the light of your Word to illuminate this nation. Let salvation come forth. Draw the evil leaders to you and do a work within their hearts.

We pray for the leaders who seek justice and search for truth. We bind the spirit of deception that would come against them. Let their pure works exceed the works of iniquity. We stand in the gap for our few good leaders. Send salvation to them and let righteousness sustain them.

We decree and declare, they shall reverence you and your glory, from the rising of the sun, unto the going down of it. You promised that you would be our covering and protection. Your Word said, 'When the enemy shall come in like a flood, the Spirit of the Lord shall lift up a standard against him.' Place your Word in their mouth. Lead and guide them into all truth. In Jesus' name, amen.

The House of Prayer

FATHER, thank you for being God! Thank you for being our father! You are a father we can trust and lean on. You are our head. You are a father, who sees, knows and cares. Your foundation is secure, and we have an assurance that you know those who are yours. We belong to you and you take care of what belongs to you. We are identified with you, and we bear your mark in our bodies.

Your house is a house of prayer. We will reverence your presence, in your house. You have made your house a defenced city, an iron pillar and brazen walls against the enemy. You have fortified your house and the congregants therein. You have promised that our enemies will fight against us, but they will not prevail, because you are with us, to deliver us.

We will not dishonor your house. Your house will not become a den of thieves. Purge our hearts as we stand before you.

We decree and declare, we will not steal, murder, commit adultery, swear falsely, or worship idol gods. When we come and stand before you in this house, which is called by your name, receive us and deliver us from ourselves. Father, we lift up the Houses of Prayer everywhere. We lift up our church family to you. Do with us that which pleases you. Sanctify the Household of Faith that your name may be there forever, and your eyes and heart might be there perpetually. Let your anointing dwell in the midst of your people. Let your glory cloud fill this house, which was built for your name. Let this house be a light that sits upon a hill. Let it be a beacon of hope for the lost and dying.

Sweep through the four corners of this house, that it might be purged of all sins against your Word. Cleanse our hearts and renew our minds. Be exalted in our midst and let your name be known among the heathen. You are God and besides you there is no other God. Glorify thyself. In Jesus' name we pray. Amen.

Righteous Judgment

FATHER, we pray for the peace of Jerusalem. They shall prosper that love them. We speak peace within the walls and prosperity within the palaces. Let them find rest within their borders that the will of God might be accomplished.

We pray for kings and those in authority. Bless us to live a quiet and peaceable life, in all godliness and honesty. Even as you watch over Israel, watch over us. You neither slumber nor sleep. Your eyes go back and forth in all the earth. You see the good and the evil. Nothing is hid from you. You are the Judge of the whole earth. No one can charge you with anything. It is you who justify, and you who condemn.

Father, in Jesus' name, we pray that those in Authority will execute righteous judgment and uphold the truth. Direct their footsteps. Don't allow them to deal falsely. Let judgment run down as waters and righteousness as a mighty stream.

We speak to the children in every household, and we say, "Stand in the good way. Ask for the old paths and walk therein. In so doing, you will find rest for your souls."

Father, we stand against deception. We will not be deceived. We will discern the voice of him who says, peace and safety, while there is a two-edged sword in his hand.

We will recognize the thief and trample him under our feet. He will not eat our harvest or our bread. He will not eat our flock or the fruit of our vines. Our sons and daughters will enjoy the blessings from God. Joy will not depart from us, for the joy of the Lord is our strength.

Father, give us a heart like yours. Help us to know you intimately. Help us to love you and serve you with our whole heart. Teach us to walk in your way, seek your face, and worship you in holiness. Let right judgments prevail in the earth. In Jesus' name we pray. Amen.

General

pray, Pray, PRAY! When you don't know what to pray, pray anyhow. The Holy Spirit will help you. We ought always pray, and not faint.

Faithful and True

FATHER, your Word is settled in heaven. I confess my sins, iniquities, transgressions, and secret faults. Your eyes are open to the righteous, and your ears are open unto our prayer.

We will bless you O Lord, our God. You spoke with your mouth and fulfilled it with your hand. You made promises to us and you fulfilled them with miracles, signs, and wonders.

There is no God like thee in heaven above or on earth beneath. You keep covenant and mercy with your children, who walk before you with all their heart.

O Lord my God, hear the prayer that your children pray before you today. Judge your children, condemn the wicked, and justify the righteous. Deliver us according to our righteousness. When we sin, turn to you and confess, then hear and forgive us.

Teach us the good way wherein we should walk. Give to every man according to his ways, because you know our heart. You only, know the hearts of all the children of men.

We will bless you because you are faithful and true. You have given rest to your children according to all that you have promised. You have been with us as you were with our forefathers. You will not leave us nor forsake us.

We pray that all the people of the earth may know, that you alone are God, and that there is none else. In Jesus' name, amen!

From Our Hearts to Heaven

FATHER, in the Name of Jesus, we offer ourselves to you, as a living sacrifice. Jesus, be the center of our lives.

In our lives be the center.
In our hearts be the center.
In our minds be the center.
In our bodies be the center.

In our decisions be the center.
In our goings and comings, be the center.
In our choices be the center.

In our homes be the center.
In our schools be the center.
On our jobs be the center.

In our present be the center.
In our future be the center.
In our dreams be the center.
In our visions be the center.
In our hopes be the center.

In our joys be the center.
In our challenges be the center.
In our friendships be the center.
In our relationships be the center.
In our fellowship be the center.

In all that we say, do, and wherever we go, be the center.

FROM OUR HEARTS, TO THE HEAVEN, JESUS BE THE CENTER!

I Will Encourage Myself

MY HEART IS FIXED, oh Lord, my heart is fixed. Lead me in the way of your wisdom. Order my footsteps as I go. Keep me from going to the left and the right. I desire to be in the center of your will, focused and steadfast. Speak your intimate desires into my heart, that I might do the things, which please you. Have pity on me, and deliver me daily from destruction.

Thank you Lord, for your loving-kindness, and tender mercies. I thank you for never leaving me or forsaking me. You have watched over your Word, to perform it in my life. Your Word is "manifested power" in my life. I walk upon my high places, because of the strength I receive from your Word. Your Word is accomplishing in me, that which you designed for me. Thank you, that my way is prosperous.

Thank you for being with me when I passed through the waters. Thank you that the rivers in my life did not drown me. And the fires did not burn me neither did the flames consume me. Thank you for the victory that overcomes the world, even my faith. My faith in you has sustained me against all odds.

Thank you Lord, for you have made me the head and not the tail. You have placed me above and not beneath. You have turned the evil that was against me into good. You have stopped the plots and plans, which were against me. And, you have turned the curses of my enemies into blessings.

I rest in the comfort of your love. I live to obey your voice. I dwell safely and securely in you. Thank you. Thank you for loving me. Thank you for wrapping your arms around me and protecting me. In the name of Jesus Christ, my Lord and Savior, I thank you for all of your blessings to me. My heart says, "Yes, and Amen!"

Let Us Pray

HEAR OUR CRY O God and attend unto our prayers!
From the ends of the earth hear the cries of your people.
There is someone, somewhere, calling on your name, asking for your mercy and needing your deliverance.
When our hearts are overwhelmed, we know nothing else to do, but to run to you for comfort. Deliver now Lord, we pray.
Father, we know that our safety is in you.
You know us and you know our hearts.
Make us upright in our hearts that we may dwell in your presence.
Let peace rest, rule, and abide in our hearts.
You are our salvation.
If there is any wicked ways in us, cleanse us and wash us through your Word.
Lord, you are our God and we believe you hear the voice of our supplications.
You are the strength of our salvation.
You have covered our heads in the day of battle.
You have established us in the earth.
Without you, we can do nothing.
In you, we live, move, and have our being.
You have always maintained the cause of your people.
You know our pathways, and you see our detours, yet, you have ordained for us to walk in victory.
We surrender to your will.
You are our refuge and our portion.
Help us to hold our peace, when the wicked is before us.
Set a watch before our mouth, and keep the doors of our lips.
Our eyes are upon you, O God; and our trust is in thee.
You promised not to leave our souls destitute.
Keep us from the snares of the enemy.
Father, in thy righteousness hear us, and in thy faithfulness answer us.
We thirst for you.
Stretch forth your hands unto us.

We stir up our pure minds, remembering all the works of thy hands.
Marvelous are thy works; the sun, moon, stars, man, and all of creation.
Cause us to see thy loving-kindness in the morning.
And cause us to know the way wherein we should walk.
Teach us to do thy will, and lead us into the depth of uprightness.
You are our light in darkness.
We will follow where you lead.
We will not walk in fear, because you are with us.
Lord, you are our fortress, our high tower, our deliverer, and our shield.
Thank you for the doors you have opened and closed for us.
We thank you for your protection from seen and unseen dangers.
Thank you Holy Spirit for dwelling within us. In Jesus' name, amen!

Our Defender

FATHER, we know that every one, who is called by your name has been created for your glory. You have commanded your sons from afar and your daughters from the ends of the earth, to be brought before thee. You even said, bring forth the blind that have eyes, and the deaf that have ears. Let all the nations be gathered together, as you declare their existence.

Father, we know that you are God! There is none that can stand against the reality of who you are. We are your witnesses. We know, believe, and understand that you alone are God. Before you, there was no God formed, and neither shall there be one after you. Beside you, there is no Saviour. There is no one who can deliver out of your hand. You perform your Word and no man can hinder you.

You are our Redeemer, the Holy One, our Creator and King. You make a way in the sea, and a path in the mighty waters. We have decided to follow you and we will not look back. We will not dwell on the former things. You promised to do a new thing in our life. You promised to make a way in our wilderness, and create rivers in our desert.

You have blotted out our transgressions. And you said you would never remember our sins again. We thank you, in Jesus' name, for the victories we have in our lives. Amen!

Steadfast and Unmovable

FATHER, we will lift up the name of Jesus. We will proclaim the greatness of our God before the heathen. You are the Rock of Ages and our Pillar to lean on. Your work is perfect and your judgments are right. You are a God of truth and righteousness. You alone have made and established us, so that we will not be moved. Let us not forsake you, the Rock of our Salvation.

We will remember the days of old, and consider the paths of our forefathers. We will trust them to make plain your ways, and to teach us the truth of our foundation. For we have an inheritance in you O God. We, your people, are your portion. Seal us with your mark.

By your grace, we ask you to lead and instruct us. Keep us as the apple of your eye. Strengthen us to walk upon the high places of the earth.

Father, please don't hide your face from us. Remember us in our low estate. Vengeance and recompense belong to you. There is no other God besides thee. You kill and you make alive. You wound and you heal. There is no one, who can deliver out of your hand.

We decree and declare, one of us will chase a thousand, and two of us will put ten thousand to flight. In the name of Jesus, we shall not be moved. Amen.

Sweet Sleep

By THE POWER and authority of the Word of God, the name of Jesus, and his shed Blood, I rebuke the tossing and turning. I cast out the irritations to my body. I come against the unhealthy racing of my mind. Devil you are defeated. I will not succumb to your torment.

These irritants do not have a right to dwell with me. They are trespassing and I cast them out now, in the mighty name of Jesus. I pull down their strongholds. And I cast down the vain imaginations. I command rest to come forth. I speak peace to my mind, comfort to my body, and rest to my spirit.

I receive the sweet sleep that God promised me in his Word. My sleep will be sweet. I will lie down and sleep. I will have dreams and see visions as God ministers to me during the night. I decree and declare, God will seal his instructions in my heart, as I rest in him.

Father, I lift up my eyes unto you. I know you see, you hear, and you care about me, and what I'm going through. I know it is your will to give me what I desire. I desire the things you desire for me. It is your will to take care of everything that concerns me. It doesn't matter to you whether it is small or great. You just want to take care of me, because you love me. Thank you for a restful night sleep. Thank you for waking up refreshed in you.

Thank you for perfecting all of the things, which concern me; in Jesus' name, amen!

The Innocent

FATHER, we lift up the hearts of the innocent ones. Those who in blind trust have been betrayed, and led to the slaughter. Let their innocence return to them speedily. Your Word said, the virgin shall rejoice with a dance, the young and old together. You promised to turn our mourning into joy. Comfort us with your love. Cause us to rejoice and not live in sorrow. Satisfy us with your goodness.

The innocent ones are taken and violated beyond imagination. They are helpless and feel there is no hope. Their questions and cries for help go unanswered. Answer them, O God! Answer the cries of the children, and hear the cries of the mothers. Hear their lamentation and bitter weeping. They are weeping for their children. They refuse to be comforted, because their children are not comforted. Wipe away their tears and reward their work. Deliver them from the hands of the enemy.

We come against human trafficking. We bind it now in the name of Jesus. We pull down the strongholds and release the spirit of conviction upon everyone the enemy is using to destroy innocent lives. We curse the monetary gain in human trafficking.

We decree and declare, children shall come again to their own border. The children shall return again. You have promised it, and it is with a certainty that we receive it, and look for it.

Father, we know that we shall all stand before your judgment seat; every man, woman and child. We will each be accountable for the deeds we have done in our bodies. Help us to be ready, we pray. In Jesus' name, amen.

Abide in Me

FATHER, let the Fruit of your Spirit be manifested in my life today. Let me show others the same love, which I have received from you. Let the joy of serving others penetrate my heart. Strengthen me to esteem others over myself. Let the joy and the rejoicing of my heart be pleasing to you.

In a world of turmoil, let peace reside within my heart. I yield myself to a spirit of harmony. I will pursue peace with all diligence. Father, fortify my spirit. I will wait patiently upon you, for you are the source of my endurance. You suffered for me, equip me to suffer for your name's sake. Teach me longsuffering.

I decree and declare I will walk with a gentle spirit. I will not be harsh or walk in rage against others. I will do that which is right and good, in your sight. I will stand on the truth of your Word. My faith shall sustain me. Let the spirit of meekness and humility rule within me.

I submit to those who have authority over me. Teach me discipline according to your Word. Let everything that I do, be in moderation and temperance. I decree I have self-control. My flesh does not dominate me, or my life. I live each day with a heart willing to forgive. You have forgiven me and taught me to forgive others. I choose to forgive. Thank you for the Fruit of your Spirit. Let it abide in me continually. In Jesus' name I pray, amen.

Remove from Me

FATHER, I lay aside all weights and the sins, which so easily cause me to stray. My heart is fixed, O Lord, my heart is fixed. I will not turn to the right or to the left. I will keep my eyes upon you.

When I am tempted to be selfish, I choose to cast down the temptation. I will consider others before I consider myself. I will seek you for directions. Your spirit will guide me in the path of righteousness. I will not be lazy or impatient. I will work in a spirit of excellence. I will complete every task you have assigned to me. Let the genuineness of my spirit be the magnet that draws others to you.

I decree and declare, dishonesty will not prevail in my heart. I chose not to be a pretender. I stand naked before thee. Examine my heart. Your Word says, where there is no vision, the people perish. Give me visions, witty inventions, and creative ideas. Open my eyes that I might see clearly.

Preserve me from poverty that I might not steal. Don't make me rich, if it will turn my heart away from you. Mold me and make me after your will. It is in the name of Jesus, I ask these things, and believe that I have received them. Amen.

Denouncing the Flesh

FATHER IN THE NAME OF JESUS, I come before you seeking refuge. I lay my body at your feet desiring to crucify my flesh. My heart's desire is to walk in your Spirit, and not fulfill the lust of my flesh. Your Word says the Spirit and the flesh are contrary to one another, so I am seeking your help to withstand the wickedness of my flesh. I need your strength. Work your will and good pleasure in me.

I come against the desires of my flesh, which seeks to draw me away from obeying your Word. I denounce all lustful works of the flesh. I call them by their names, and I decree and declare that they have no power over me.

I speak to the spirit of adultery, fornication, uncleanness, lasciviousness, idolatry, witchcraft, hatred, variance, emulations, wrath, strife, seditions, heresies, envying, murders, drunkenness, partying, and the like, I command everyone of you to flee from my presence, in the name of Jesus. I do not yield any member of my body to you. I denounce you and your presence in my life.

I decree and declare, vain imaginations and foolishness will not darken my heart. I will not dishonor my body in any way. I will not be influenced or controlled with vile unnatural affections. I will not be unrighteous, wicked, covetous, malicious, or deceitful in my heart.

I decree and declare that I am not a whisperer, backbiter, boaster, or a covenant breaker; and I am obedient to my parents.

I cast down vain imaginations and every high thing that exalts itself against the knowledge of God. I bring into captivity every thought to the obedience of Christ.

I decree and declare, I am living a clean and pure life before God. Thank you Lord for victory through the blood of Jesus Christ. Amen.

To God Be the Glory

"Thus saith the LORD, Let not the wise man glory in his wisdom, neither let the mighty man glory in his might, let not the rich man glory in his riches: But let him that glorieth glory in this, that he understandeth and knoweth me, that I am the LORD which exercise loving-kindness, judgment, and righteousness, in the earth: for in these things I delight, saith the LORD." (Jeremiah 9:23-24)

As we pray and develop our intimate relationship with God, the glory of our latter house will become greater than of the former, and we will have peace in our midst. The peace that only the God of Peace can give.

When God has granted us all of our petitions, and we are walking in the blessings, and the impact of our suffering no longer has the sting, let us not forget God!

I pray that God makes each of us perfect in every good work. Equip us to do his will, and work in us that which is pleasing in his sight. To whom we give glory, forever and ever. Amen.

pray, Pray, PRAY

ABRAHAM RECEIVED A PROMISE FROM GOD. He prayed according to the promise he had received. When he was old, one the promise concerning his seed had not yet been fulfilled, so he prayed with his servant and told him to do whatever was necessary to keep the promise alive, until it was manifested. The servant prayed. His prayer signifies he may not have known the God of his master, but he knew the power of prayer. He starts by saying, "O Lord God of my master Abraham, I pray thee, send me good speed this day, and show kindness unto my master Abraham." Their prayers were answered. Yet, after receiving the answer, the servant prayed again. He bowed his head and worshipped God. He said, "Blessed be the Lord God of my master Abraham, who hath not left destitute my master of his mercy and his truth: I being in the way, the Lord led me to the house of my master's brethren." Pray, pray, pray! Don't stop praying and believing.

We should pray before, during, and after every situation we face in life. If we pray morning, noon and night, it will keep us connected to God. We become sensitive to His voice and we learn His heart. Pray, pray, pray.

God's Word reminds us that man born of a woman is of a few days and full of trouble, so we must pray. The Word encourages us to always pray, so we won't faint. When I was young, they use to sing a song, "Down on my knees when trouble rise, I'll talk to Jesus beyond the skies. He promised me He would hear my plea, if I would tell Him down on my knees." I believe this is where our disconnection occurred. We conditioned ourselves to pray when we were in trouble, but we lost sight of the other two times, the good time and all the time. Pray, pray, pray!

We are told to trust in the Lord with all our heart, and lean not unto our own understanding. In all our ways we are to acknowledge Him and He promised to direct our paths. God works and no man can hinder Him. Yet, it seems we believe our panic will get Him to move quicker than our trust. When the truth is, He's looking for us to trust Him rather than panic.

When the disciples were in the midst of a storm, the wind and waves covered the ship. Jesus was sleeping and His disciples woke Him saying, "Lord, save us, we perish." Before Jesus answered their prayer, He rebuked them because of their lack of trust and faith in Him.

Afterwards, He answered their prayer immediately. Their life situation was changed in an instant. Yet, valuable time was wasted. The time it took Jesus to address their fears and doubts, was time they could have been experiencing peace and calm. Indulge me! I can imagine the disciples thinking, "Why do we need this conversation right now? If He continue talking we are going to die." Jesus knew His time with the disciples was limited, so he used every life situation as a platform for a teachable moment. Likewise, we should consider the lesson associated with each of our life situations. Let's look at a couple of them.

At midnight, while locked up in jail, Paul and Silas prayed and sang praises unto God. Suddenly and immediately two things happened. The first thing that happened appears terrible, because it looks like things are going from bad to worst. They were already innocent men locked up in jail, and now suddenly a GREAT earthquake hits. But the second thing occurred immediately. Immediately, all of the prison doors were opened and Paul and Silas' bands were untied.

Prayer and praise became the nucleus in their bad situation, and the Word of God was manifested in their lives at that moment. "...all things work together for good to them that love God, to them who are the called according to his purpose." Pray, pray, pray!

Their situation reminded me of another song from my youth, "Don't stop praying, the Lord is nigh, don't stop praying, He'll hear your cry, the Lord has promised, and His Word is true, don't stop praying, He'll answer you."

If we look into the Scriptures, we will see the many times God heard and answered the prayers of His children; i.e., "and they cried unto the Lord" …He heard them. He came and looked upon them. He spoke to them." In an instant, in one day, in the same hour, God changed situations in people's lives.

There are some difficulties in our lives, which we created. We did it to ourselves! And more often than not, whatever we did was a result of disobedience. In Acts 27, Paul warned those in charge that they should not take the voyage because of the potential danger. The leaders rejected Paul's advice and did what the important people recommended.

If we are going to make it, we must pray. And if we are going to pray, we must align ourselves with people who have a passion for God and a dependency on God's guidance. They can be smarter than you or not as smart as you, but they should have a passion to obey God. You don't need anyone who is going to give you:

Sympathy instead of God's Word
Opinions instead of Prayer
Compassion instead of Truth

As warned by Paul, the people in the ship found themselves in the midst of a storm. The South wind saying, "this is my turf"; the tempestuous wind saying, "no it's not, this is my turf"; and the ship was caught in the middle, being tossed to and fro. They were in a hopeless situation and threw up their hands in desperation. However, if we pray like Abraham, who against hope believed in hope and staggered not at the promise of God, we will live victorious lives.

I learned how to pray because my mom loved me enough to take me to church. As we prepared to pray, everyone walked to the Altar singing. We sang one song over and over again. The song was:

Oh, oh Lord, have mercy.
Oh, oh Lord, have mercy.
Oh, oh Lord, have mercy.
Have mercy, mercy on me!

Oh, oh Lord, I need thee.
Oh, oh Lord, I need thee.
Oh, oh Lord, I need thee.
Have mercy, mercy on me!

We sang that song the entire time, during and after, the congregation gathered around the Altar. We sang it so much that by the time for prayer, my spirit was already broken and it was easy to be transparent before the Lord.

Don't misunderstand me, there are times when I am in the midst of my storm and I want to come out swinging. My flesh wants to retaliate. There are times when I throw up my hands because I feel enough is enough, but God still requires me to surrender. In those times when I want to punch my adversary where it hurts, prayer inspires me to let God handle it. God will fight for us. We don't need to fight the battles that belong to God. Our battle is in our commitment to pray, pray, pray.

Pray His Word! Pray His Promises! Pray His many Acts. Let us pray, pray, pray!

Books Written by Rena Boston

Walking Softly I   **$12.95**

A book of poetry designed to help keep love alive. It creates an intimate ambiance to discuss ugly issues and helps men and women express their feelings. It brings warmth to ice cold settings. This book is a must read… (June 2003)

Walking Softly II   **$12.95**

Part Two of the Walking Softly Book Collection reveals new ideas to invigorate your relationship. It is for anyone who is "in love", waiting "for love", and those who are not sure "about love". (August 2004)

Jehovah, It's All About You Book   **$7.95**

Have you ever been Center-Stage with God? Use this book during your devotions and it will move you into a powerful worship experience with God. (September 2004)

Jehovah, It's All About You CD   **$15.00**

This CD contains the Jehovah worship book PLUS several worship songs intermittently sung by renown artist Kenneth L. Daniel. Allow this CD to move you into a powerful worship experience with God. (June 2005)

"If Only" Motivational CD   **$7.00**

Have you ever made excuses you knew were unacceptable? After all, self-preservation is all about excuses; our reasons and justifications for "doing" and "saying"; what we do and say. Listen to this CD and stop allowing excuses to stunt your growth. (June 2005)

Walking Softly Calendar   **$12.95**

This calendar contains 12 poems surrounding love-walking. The power to feel love, find love, and experience love are on every page. The monthly challenges are designed to create an atmosphere of sensitivity and warmth. (October 2005)

Just Writers Publishing Company
Where Fingers Write From the Heart

*Prices do not include Shipping & Handling.

Books Written by Rena Boston

Humility Before Honour $19.95
This hardcover book is a must-read. It is a "keepsake" for generations to come. Bishop Carlis Lee Moody, Sr's biography will reveal a man of faith and integrity. He has travelled the globe fulfilling the great commission in over 42 countries. He is an international symbol of hope to those he serves. (October 2005)

Walking Softly for Everyone $14.95
This book contains a special message for everyone. It encourages the discouraged, cautions the singles, massages the heart of the divorced, and prepares the married for a life of challenge and love. (April 2007)

Hopes, Dreams, Visions $9.95
This motivational handbook revitalizes the heart and provides the strength to conquer obstacles in life. It contains 60 scenarios designed to elevate the readers' expectations of themselves. (August 2013)

Money, The Master or The Servant $8.95
This book is a must-read! However, you may find yourself laughing and crying at the same time. It may even feel like a roller coaster ride, but I assure you there's a safe landing. It is designed to motivate you to become the Master of your Money and sharpen your awareness of money's proper place as a Servant. Learn how to allow your money to serve you. As you stroll with me on this debt- free journey, you will experience a liberation and a thirst to assume control of your money immediately. The primary goal of this book is to encourage you to begin your debt-free journey by managing your money wisely. (October 2014)

No Scars $11.95
Raven was on the verge of insanity; yet, she escaped with 'No Scars'. The evidence of her sufferings was wiped away. It was so dramatic that it was almost unbelievable. Slowly stepping forward, Raven contemplated her image in the mirror. The reflection she saw and its persona overwhelmed her. She did not look like what she had gone through! She didn't even look like her original image, she was better! (January 2015)

Just Writers Publishing Company
"Where Fingers Write From the Heart"

*Prices do not include Shipping & Handling.

Prayer List

Prayer List

_____

_____

_____

_____

_____

_____

_____

_____

_____

_____

_____

_____

_____

_____

_____

_____

_____

_____

_____

_____

_____

Prayer List

_____

_____

_____

_____

_____

_____

_____

_____

_____

_____

_____

_____

_____

_____

_____

_____

_____

_____

_____

_____

_____

_____

_____

Prayer List

_____
_____
_____
_____
_____
_____
_____
_____
_____
_____
_____
_____
_____
_____
_____
_____
_____
_____
_____
_____
_____

www.ingramcontent.com/pod-product-compliance
Lightning Source LLC
LaVergne TN
LVHW041218080426
835508LV00011B/990